THE SHAKESPEARE PARALLEL TEXT SERIES

MACBETH

Edited by
Daniel Leary
The City College of New York

THE PERFECTION FORM COMPANY
LOGAN, IOWA

Special contents of this edition
Copyright © 1983 by
THE PERFECTION FORM COMPANY
1000 North Second Avenue
Logan, Iowa 51546

Copyright © 1975 by
SIMON & SCHUSTER, INC.

All rights reserved

A NOTE FROM THE PUBLISHER

The purpose of the Parallel Text Series of Shakespeare's plays is to assist the reader in understanding and appreciating the work of the foremost poet and dramatist of the English language. That there are considerable difficulties in reading and understanding this language is apparent from a casual glance through the many modern editions of the plays, which are accompanied by copious notes on each page of the text. Even these heavily annotated editions often fail to go far enough in illuminating the richly poetic and elliptical language that in large part demonstrates Shakespeare's genius and primacy, and constitutes our frequent perplexity.

In providing a line-by-line, contemporary prose paraphrase of the play on facing pages we have, in a sense, merely carried the convention of using explanatory notes to its logical conclusion. No attempt has been made to translate Shakespeare into modern poetry — a presumptuous and virtually impossible task. Instead, we have tried to render the often unfamiliar and remote Elizabethan language into a neutral and comprehensible modern equivalent. By its very nature, this task sometimes neglects the richness and complexity of the text, which is, in part, created by Shakespeare's magnificent and original use of language. Thus, the paraphrase is offered as an aid to understanding, not as a substitute for reading the original. The reader will find that referring to the paraphrase will often clarify the surface of the text, but the rewards to be found in reading Shakespeare yield themselves only to the careful and dedicated student of the original.

The Past is Prologue

Shakespeare lives! So writes his most eminent biographer, S. Schoenbaum, in the prologue to *Shakespeare: The Globe and the World* (New York: Oxford University Press, 1979). And the evidence is all around us.

We find it in the language we use. When we lament that "the course of true love never did run smooth," whether we are conscious of it or not, we are quoting from *A Midsummer Night's Dream*. When we observe that a well-intended law or regulation is "more honor'd in the breach than the observance," we are applying — or perhaps misapplying — a phrase from *Hamlet*. When we inscribe "What's past is prologue" on the National Archives building in our nation's capital, we are dignifying a minor line from *The Tempest*. Often without realizing it, we find ourselves speaking, if only momentarily, in the accents of a Portia or a Polonius, a Macbeth or a Mercutio. And when we *do* realize it — when we are conscious of the Shakespearean idiom embedded in so much of our daily speech — we take pleasure in those subtle turns of phrase that continue to enrich our discourse. A veteran gardener recently observed, for example, that anyone who calls a rose by any other name has probably been pruning.

Alongside the Greek classics and the King James version of the Bible, Shakespeare's words and works offer a cultural treasure chest from which English-speaking peoples have been drawing, in one way or another, for more than three and a half centuries. Folks have been

following the advice given in *Kiss Me Kate* — brushing up on their Shakespeare — for quite some time.

But Shakespeare's presence is also reflected in a number of other ways. Consider, for example, the more than 800 operatic and symphonic compositions deriving from such plays as *The Merry Wives of Windsor*, *The Taming of the Shrew*, and *Othello*. Or Broadway musicals, such as *The Boys from Syracuse* (a take-off on *The Comedy of Errors*) and *West Side Story* (Leonard Bernstein's New York gang-war updating of *Romeo and Juliet*). Or literary works such as William Faulkner's *The Sound and the Fury*, a sustained allusion to Macbeth's "tomorrow and tomorrow and tomorrow" speech. Here in the United States, Shakespeare has been part of our lives since the earliest days of the republic — even on the frontier, where spinoffs and parodies of Shakespeare helped while away many an hour in the nineteenth century. We've all delighted in the fractured Shakespeare offered up by the Duke and the King in Mark Twain's *Huckleberry Finn*. Ah yes, numerous — but not always sweet — are the uses of Shakespeare.

Nor is there any reason to think that Shakespeare's influence will be any less vital in the future than in the past. In most of the countries of the world, Shakespeare continues to maintain his position as the most frequently performed playwright. Every summer in the United States, for example, Shakespeare festivals highlight the vacation map from Maine to Texas, from Alabama to Oregon.

Ben Jonson was right, then, when he prefaced the first collected edition of Shakespeare's plays with the words "he was not of an age, but for all time!"

The Stratford Years

But if Shakespeare was a man for all time, he was also very much a man of his own age. Christened at Holy Trinity Church in Stratford-upon-Avon in April, 1564, he grew up, the son of illiterate parents, in a small Warwickshire town more noted for its wool and leather goods than for its literary cultivation. His mother, Mary Arden, was the daughter of a well-to-do farmer. His father, John Shakespeare, was a successful glovemaker who held several important borough offices in Stratford before he suffered financial reverses during William's teen years. The birthplace house still stands.

It seems all but certain that young Shakespeare spent most of his weekdays at the nearby Stratford grammar school, where, having learned his ABCs and the Lord's Prayer from a hornbook, he would have gone on to study Latin

Holy Trinity Church, Stratford-on-Avon

Shakespeare's House, Stratford-on-Avon

under the supervision of a stern schoolmaster.
Sundays he would have attended religious
services, studying the catechism of the newly
re-established Church of England and worshiping
in accordance with *The Book of Common Prayer*.

It was a rigorous upbringing, and it equipped
Shakespeare with enough background to become
one of the most widely educated men who ever
lived — despite the fact that he never attended a
day at a college or university.

Judging from his plays and poems, we may
infer that Shakespeare was interested in virtually
every aspect of human life — in professions such
as law, medicine, religion, and teaching; in everyday occupations such as farming, sheepherding,
tailoring, and shopkeeping; in skills such as
fishing, gardening, and cooking. Much of what
Shakespeare knew about these and countless
other subjects he would have acquired from
books. He must have been a voracious reader.

But he would have learned a great deal, also, from simply being alert to all that went on around him. He would have observed the plant and animal life of the nearby woods that he would later immortalize, in *As You Like It*, as the Forest of Arden. While there, he may have hunted from time to time; one legend has it that he left Stratford because he had been caught poaching deer from the estate of a powerful squire four miles upstream. He probably learned to swim as a youth, skinny-dipping in the river Avon. He may have participated in the kinds of athletic competition that were popular in the Elizabethan equivalent of the Olympics, the Cotswold Games. Chances are, too, that he would have been familiar with indoor recreations such as hazard (a popular dice game), or chess, or any of a number of card games. His works make it clear that he was fully at home with a broad spectrum of pastimes characteristic of the daily life of Elizabethan England.

Once his schooldays ended, Shakespeare married, at the age of eighteen, a woman who was eight years his senior. Anne Hathaway was pregnant when the wedding vows were solemnized. That it was a forced marriage is unlikely. But we shall never know how close the couple were. What we do know is that a daughter, Susanna, was baptized in Holy Trinity in May of 1583, followed less than two years later by the christening of twins, Hamnet and Judith. Sometime thereafter, certainly by the late 1580s, the father was in London.

The London Years

London was approximately a hundred miles distant. Shakespeare may have traveled there by way of the spires of Oxford, as do most visitors returning from Stratford to London today. But why he went, or when, history does not tell us. It has been plausibly suggested that he joined an acting troupe that was one player short when it toured Stratford in 1587. All we know for certain is that by 1592 Shakespeare had established himself as an actor and had written at least three plays. One of these — the third part of *Henry VI* — was alluded to in that year in a testament by a dying poet and playwright. Robert Greene warned his fellow playwrights to beware of the "upstart crow" who, not content with being a mere player, was aspiring to a share of the livelihood that had previously been the exclusive province of professional writers such as "the University Wits."

If we look at what Shakespeare had written by the early 1590s, we see that he had already become thoroughly familiar with the daily round of what was rapidly developing into one of the great capitals of Europe. Shakespeare knew St. Paul's Cathedral, famous not only as a house of worship but also as the marketplace where books were bought and sold. He knew the Inns of Court, where aspiring young lawyers studied for the bar. He knew the river Thames,

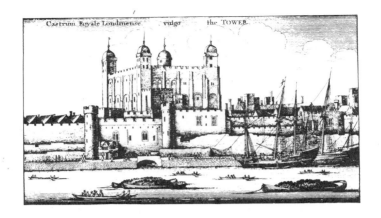

Castrum Royale Londinense   vulgo   the TOWER

spanned by the ever-busy, ever-fascinating
London Bridge. He knew the Tower, where so
many of the characters he would depict in his
history plays had met their deaths, and where in
his own lifetime, such prominent noblemen as the
Earl of Essex and Sir Walter Raleigh would be
imprisoned prior to their executions. He knew
Westminster, where Parliament met when sum-
moned by the Queen, and where the Queen
herself kept her court at Whitehall Palace. He
knew the harbor, where English ships, having
won control of the seas by defeating the "invinci-
ble" Spanish Armada in 1588, had begun in
earnest to explore the New World.

In Shakespeare's day, London was a vigorous
city of approximately 160,000. If in its more
majestic aspects it was dominated by the court of
Queen Elizabeth — the sovereign most historians
regard as the greatest monarch in English
history — in its everyday affairs it was accented
by the hustle-bustle of getting and spending. Its
Royal Exchange was one of the forerunners of
today's stock exchanges. Its many marketplaces
offered a variety of goods for a variety of tastes.

Its crowded streets presented a colorful pageant of Elizabethan modes of transport and dress, ranging from countrywomen in homespun to elegant ladies in apparel as decorative as their husbands' wealth — and the Queen's edicts on clothing — would allow. Its inns and taverns afforded a robust diversity of vivid personalities— eating, drinking, talking, and enjoying games of all kinds.

London was, in short, a stimulating social and cultural environment for the poet whose works would later be praised as the very "mirror of life." And the young playwright took full advantage of the opportunity to observe humanity in all its facets. Without the broadening that London provided, it is doubtful that Shakespeare could ever have created such breathtakingly real characters as Falstaff, Prince Hal, and "all the good lads in Eastcheap."

Not that all was always well. Like any major city, London also had its unpleasant aspects. For one thing, it was riddled with conflict. Preachers were constantly denouncing the excessive use of cosmetics by women of the period. Even Hamlet speaks out against "your paintings," telling Ophelia "God has given you one face, and you make yourselves another."

In a similar vein, the city's Puritan authorities, regarding the theatres as dens of iniquity, closed them down on any available pretext, particularly during periods when the plague was rampant.

But even with the theatres closed, London was not free of vice and crime. In the Bankside district, prostitution abounded, as did gambling and drunkenness. Pickpockets, vagabonds, and other members of the fraternity of urban lowlife lay in wait for "conies" or unsuspecting victims. With so many "notorious villainies" for the "Belman of London" to bring to light, it is not surprising that some of the most interesting pamphlets of the period were muckraking tracts from reformers outraged by the sinfulness of the modern metropolis.

In such a setting did Shakespeare write and perform the greatest dramatic works the world has ever seen. And he did so in an area of the city that was accustomed to entertainments we would regard as the very antithesis of the sweet Swan of Avon's poetic sublimity. For if Bankside was to blossom into the finest theatrical center of that or any other age, it was also, for better or worse, the seedbed for such crude and cruel spectator sports as bear-baiting, bull-baiting, and cock-fighting. This may help account for the blood and violence one often sees on the Elizabethan stage, even in such Shakespearean works as *Titus Andronicus*, *Julius Caesar*, and *King Lear*.

S. PAULES CHURCH

Bow Church

Guild Hall

The Eoll Schipes

THAMESIS

The 9 Golly fight

The Bear Gardne

The Globe

But of course there was more than murder and
mayhem in the "wooden O" that served as
amphitheatre for Shakespeare's works. On a
stage largely devoid of scenery, the playwright
and the actor made splendid use of language and
gesture to establish locale, atmosphere, and
meaning. And because the stage was surrounded
on three sides by nearby spectators, the
playwright and the actor benefited from a more
intimate relationship with the audience than is
customary in present-day theatres fitted with a
curtain and a proscenium arch. For Shakespeare,
this meant that he could allow a character to con-
fide in the audience through asides, as does Iago
in *Othello*, or to be overheard as he meditates in
solitude, as does Hamlet in his celebrated "To be
or not to be" soliloquy.

The limitations of the Globe and similar Elizabethan theatres are obvious to us today. For one thing, they were exposed to the sky and thus could not operate comfortably in inclement weather or in darkness. For another, lacking spotlights and other modern paraphernalia, they could not achieve some of the special effects we have come to take for granted in the theatre of our own day. What we sometimes forget, however, is that these limitations could be liberating for the playwright and the actor, making possible a kind of dramatic invention and flexibility difficult to duplicate in the more "advanced" theatre of the twentieth century.

The same was probably true in the Blackfriars and other private indoor theatres of the period, not to mention the halls at Court or the great palaces of the nobility. For it is well to remember that many of Shakespeare's plays were performed in theatrical settings other than the Globe, or its predecessor, the Theatre, or other amphitheatres of the period. Shakespeare's company was known as the Lord Chamberlain's Men from 1594 to 1603, when Queen Elizabeth died; after the accession of King James I, from 1603 on, it was known as the King's Men. Both designations implied a special relationship with the Court, and Shakespeare and his colleagues were invited to perform before the monarch more often than all the other acting troupes in the realm combined.

Shakespeare's real bread and butter, however, came from the immense cross section of the English populace who thronged to Bankside to see his plays performed. Despite the occasional caviling of such rival playwrights as Ben Jonson (whose admiration for Shakespeare was at times "this side idolatry"), we have reason to believe

Interior of Holy Trinity Church

that Shakespeare's dramatic works were immediately recognized for their artistic merits. By 1598, a critic named Francis Meres was comparing Shakespeare's genius to that of the greatest poets of antiquity — Ovid, Plautus, and Seneca — and finding the contemporary playwright superior to his classical predecessors. But unlike many great writers, Shakespeare was also a popular success in his own lifetime. He earned a generous amount of money, invested it wisely in real estate, both in London and in Stratford, and around 1613, eased into a gentleman's retirement — the owner of New Place, the second largest house in his native town.

There, three years later, he died. Fittingly, his death date, like the date tradition has agreed upon for his birth date, was April 23, the day England celebrated its patron saint. In the four centuries since the poet's birth, it seems no exaggeration to say that he has eclipsed even the heroic St. George in glory.

Epilogue

Shakespeare was laid to rest where fifty-two years earlier he had been christened. Shortly thereafter, a monument to his memory was erected above the tomb in Holy Trinity, and that monument is still in place for Shakespeare admirers to see today. But an even greater monument to his memory was produced several years later, when his theatrical colleagues assembled a large volume of his plays. The First Folio of 1623 was a labor of love, compiled as "an office to the dead, to procure his orphans' guardians" and "to keep the memory of so worthy a friend and fellow alive as was our Shakespeare." To that end, it was an unparalleled success, a publication that has aptly been summed up as "incomparably the most important work in the English language."

Among other things, the First Folio preserves what is generally considered the most reliable portrait of Shakespeare, the title-page engraving by Martin Droeshout. In dedicatory verses opposite the portrait, Ben Jonson attests to its authenticity. But quite properly, he then goes on to observe that though the engraver has "hit his face," he has been unable to draw "his wit." For that — for the mastery of language, of character, of poetic drama, of all that reminds us that, after all is said and done, "the play's the thing" — Jonson tells the reader, "look not on his picture but his book."

And so, for more than three and a half centuries, we have. We have read, and studied, and memorized, and performed — and yes, we have worshiped — the man Jonson praised as "Soul of the Age! The applause, delight, the wonder of our stage!"

Bardolatry — the word we use to refer to Shakespeare-worship — has had many manifestations over the intervening centuries. It has animated hundreds of Shakespeare festivals and celebrations, of which undoubtedly the most famous was the great Shakespeare Jubilee of 1769. On that occasion, thousands braved rainy Stratford weather to participate in ceremonies presided over by the principal actor of the eighteenth century, David Garrick. In a somewhat inverted form, Bardolatry has given rise to the notion that someone other than the son of ill-educated, small-town parents wrote the plays we attribute to William Shakespeare. Hence Francis Bacon, the Earl of Oxford, and other members of the nobility have been proposed as the "true" author of the works we still securely hold to be Shakespeare's. And Bardolatry has also occasioned an unceasing cavalcade of Shakespearean curios and knickknacks: everything from ceramic figurines and mulberry-wood chests to Shakespeare-lovers' poker cloths and Superbard T-shirts.

On the more serious side, appreciation of Shakespeare has inspired notable works of art by painters as diverse as Thomas Rowlandson, George Romney, Henry Fuseli, Eugene Delacroix, George Cruikshank, Arthur Rackham, Pablo Picasso, Salvador Dali, and David Hockney. His works have provided the basis of hundreds of musical tributes, by composers ranging from Beethoven to Mendelssohn, Tchaikovsky to Verdi. And of course his plays continue to be performed in theatres, in movie houses, and on television screens.

The Bard is in our bones. Shakespeare lives.

John F. Andrews
Former Editor Shakespeare Quarterly
Folger Shakespeare Library

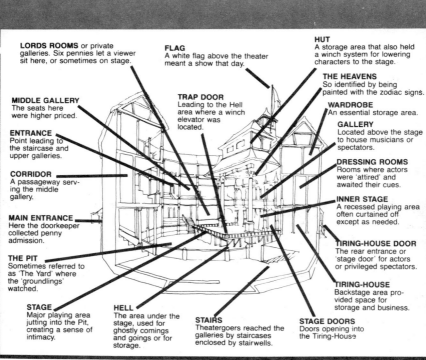

LORDS ROOMS or private galleries. Six pennies let a viewer sit here, or sometimes on stage.

FLAG
A white flag above the theater meant a show that day.

HUT
A storage area that also held a winch system for lowering characters to the stage.

MIDDLE GALLERY
The seats here were higher priced.

TRAP DOOR
Leading to the Hell area where a winch elevator was located.

THE HEAVENS
So identified by being painted with the zodiac signs.

WARDROBE
An essential storage area.

ENTRANCE
Point leading to the staircase and upper galleries.

GALLERY
Located above the stage to house musicians or spectators.

CORRIDOR
A passageway serving the middle gallery.

DRESSING ROOMS
Rooms where actors were 'attired' and awaited their cues.

MAIN ENTRANCE
Here the doorkeeper collected penny admission.

INNER STAGE
A recessed playing area often curtained off except as needed.

THE PIT
Sometimes referred to as 'The Yard' where the 'groundlings' watched.

TIRING-HOUSE DOOR
The rear entrance or 'stage door' for actors or privileged spectators.

TIRING-HOUSE
Backstage area provided space for storage and business.

STAGE
Major playing area jutting into the Pit, creating a sense of intimacy.

HELL
The area under the stage, used for ghostly comings and goings or for storage.

STAIRS
Theatergoers reached the galleries by staircases enclosed by stairwells.

STAGE DOORS
Doors opening into the Tiring-House

MACBETH

Orson Welles as Macbeth makes final arrangements with the murderers in his film version of *Macbeth*.

Macbeth

Act I, Scene i: [*An open place.*] *Thunder and lightning. Enter Three Witches.*

FIRST WITCH
  When shall we three meet again?
  In thunder, lightning, or in rain?

SECOND WITCH
  When the hurlyburly's done,
  When the battle's lost and won.

THIRD WITCH
5 That will be ere the set of sun.

FIRST WITCH
  Where the place?

SECOND WITCH
                Upon the heath*

THIRD WITCH
  There to meet with Macbeth.

FIRST WITCH
  I come, Graymalkin.*

SECOND WITCH
  Paddock* calls.

THIRD WITCH
                Anon!

ALL
10 Fair is foul, and foul is fair.
  Hover through the fog and filthy air.
    Exeunt.

---

6 *heath* barren, open country, covered with small shrubs.
8 *Graymalkin* gray cat. This is the "familiar" or attendant spirit of the

2

Macbeth

Act I, Scene i: A barren heath in Scotland. Thunder and lightning.
Enter Three Witches.

FIRST WITCH
  When shall we three meet again?
  Will it be during thunder, lightning, or rain?

SECOND WITCH
  When the turmoil's over,
  when the battle is lost by one side and won by another.

THIRD WITCH
  That will be before sunset.

FIRST WITCH
  Where will we meet?

SECOND WITCH
  On the heath.

THIRD WITCH
  It's there we'll meet Macbeth.

FIRST WITCH
  My cat, Graymalkin, calls. I come.

SECOND WITCH
  My frog, Paddock, calls.

THIRD WITCH
  Coming!

ALL
  The beautiful is ugly and the ugly is beautiful.
  Let us fly through the fog and the filthy air.
    They exit.

First Witch.
  9 *Paddock* a toad. It is the "familiar" of the Second Witch.

Scene ii: [A military camp.] Alarum within. Enter King [DUNCAN], MALCOLM, DONALBAIN, LENNOX, *with Attendants, meeting a bleeding Sergeant.*

KING
What bloody man is that? He can report,
As seemeth by his plight, of the revolt
The newest state.

MALCOLM
              This is the sergeant*
Who like a good and hardy soldier fought
5   'Gainst my captivity. Hail, brave friend!
Say to the king the knowledge of the broil
As thou didst leave it.

CAPTAIN
              Doubtful it stood,
As two spent swimmers, that do cling together
And choke their art. The merciless Macdonwald—
10   Worthy to be a rebel for to that
The multiplying villainies of nature
Do swarm upon him—from the Western Isles
Of kerns and gallowglasses is supplied;
And Fortune,* on his damnèd quarrel smiling,
15   Showed like a rebel's whore: but all's too weak:
For brave Macbeth—well he deserves that name—
Disdaining Fortune, with his brandished steel,
Which smoked with bloody execution,
Like valor's minion carved out his passage
20   Till he faced the slave;
Which ne'er shook hands, nor bade farewell to him,
Till he unseamed him from the nave to th' chops,
And fixed his head upon our battlements.

KING
O valiant cousin! Worthy gentleman!

CAPTAIN
25   As whence the sun 'gins his reflection
Shipwracking storms and direful thunders break,

---

3 *sergeant* a much higher rank than a modern sergeant. He was probably a knight or squire and thus could be called "Captain" in the stage directions.

Act I, Scene ii: A military camp. A call to arms is sounded off-stage. KING DUNCAN *enters accompanied by his sons,* MALCOLM *and* DONALBAIN, *with* LENNOX *and other Attendants. Enter a bleeding Captain from the other side of the stage.*

KING

Who is that blood-stained man? He can tell us—
as it seems from his appearance—about the latest
    developments of
the rebellion.

MALCOLM

This is the officer,
who, like a good, rugged soldier, fought
5 to prevent my being captured. Greetings, brave friend!
Tell the King about the status of the battle
when you left it.

CAPTAIN

The outcome was as uncertain
as two exhausted swimmers who hang on to one another
and pull each other down. The merciless Macdonwald—
10 well suited to be a rebel, since
all the swelling, sinister forces of nature
seem to be attracted to him from the Hebrides—
was supplied with both light and heavy armed infantry.
And good luck, smiling on the rebel's damned cause,
15 acted like his whore (and made love to him). But it was not
    enough.
Brave Macbeth—and he well deserves to be called brave—
scorning Macdonwald's good luck and waving his sword,
which steamed from its bloody deeds,
Macbeth, the very darling of bravery itself, carved out a
    passage before him
20 until he faced the slave, Macdonwald.
And Macbeth never shook hands nor said farewell to Macdonwald
until he had ripped him open from the stomach to the jaws
and stuck his head on top of our castle's wall.

KING

O valiant kinsman! Noble gentleman!

CAPTAIN

25 As from the east where the sun rises
come ship-wrecking storms and dreadful thunder,

---

14 *Fortune* the personified power which determines human success, distributing happiness and unhappiness according to her own whims, showing some favor to all men but being constant to none.

So from that spring whence comfort seemed to come
Discomfort swells. Mark, King of Scotland, mark:
No sooner justice had, with valor armed,
30   Compelled these skipping kerns to trust their heels,
But the Norweyan lord, surveying vantage,
With furbished arms and new supplies of men,
Began a fresh assault.

KING
                    Dismayed not this
Our captains, Macbeth and Banquo?

CAPTAIN
                                   Yes,
35   As sparrows eagles, or the hare the lion.
If I say sooth, I must report they were
As cannons overcharged with double cracks;
So they doubly redoubled strokes upon the foe.
Except they meant to bathe in reeking wounds,
40   Or memorize another Golgotha,*
I cannot tell—
But I am faint; my gashes cry for help.

KING
So well thy words become thee as thy wounds;
They smack of honor both. Go get him surgeons.
                    [*Exit Captain, attended.*]
                    Enter ROSS *and* ANGUS.
Who comes here?

MALCOLM
45   The worthy Thane* of Ross.

LENNOX
What a haste looks through his eyes! So should he look
That seems to speak things strange.

ROSS
                                   God save the King!

KING
Whence cam'st thou, worthy thane?

ROSS
                                   From Fife, great King;
Where the Norweyan banners flout the sky
50   And fan our people cold.

---

40   *Golgotha*   Calvary, the "place of skulls" where Christ was crucified.
45   *Thane*   an old Scottish title for the chief of a clan, roughly equal
to "earl."

so the little stream that looks so pleasant
can swell into raging water. Note, King of Scotland, note well:
no sooner had justice, armed with courage,

30   forced these cowardly troops into a hasty retreat,
than the Norwegian lord, seeing an opportunity,
with new weapons and fresh reserves
began a new attack.

KING

Didn't this frighten
our captains, Macbeth and Banquo?

CAPTAIN

Yes,

35   as sparrows frighten eagles, or the rabbit the lion.
To tell the truth, I must report that Macbeth and Banquo were
like cannons loaded with double charges of explosives,
so that they quadrupled their assault on the enemy.
Unless they meant to bathe in the steaming blood of the
    wounded,

40   or make the place memorable as a second Golgotha,
I cannot tell—
but I am faint; my wounds demand attention.

KING

Your words suit you as well as your wounds
and both have the taste of manly honor. Go get him surgeons.
    Exit Captain with attendants.
    Enter ROSS *and* ANGUS.
Who comes here?

MALCOLM

45   The noble Thane of Ross.

LENNOX

How eager he looks. He seems to be a man
who has strange things to tell.

ROSS

God save the King!

KING

Where did you come from, noble thane?

ROSS

From Fife, great King,
where the Norwegian banners disgrace our sky

50   and chill our people with fear.

Norway himself, with terrible numbers,
Assisted by that most disloyal traitor
The Thane of Cawdor, began a dismal conflict;
Till that Bellona's* bridegroom, lapped in proof,
55   Confronted him with self-comparisons,
Point against point, rebellious arm 'gainst arm,
Curbing his lavish spirit; and, to conclude,
The victory fell on us.

KING
                              Great happiness!

ROSS
                                        That now
Sweno, the Norways' king, craves composition;
60   Nor would we deign him burial of his men
Till he disbursèd, at Saint Colme's Inch,*
Ten thousand dollars* to our general use.

KING
No more that Thane of Cawdor shall deceive
Our bosom interest. Go pronounce his present death,
65   And with his former title greet Macbeth.

ROSS
I'll see it done.

KING
What he hath lost, noble Macbeth hath won.
        Exeunt.

Scene iii: [*A heath.*] *Thunder. Enter the Three Witches.*

FIRST WITCH
Where hast thou been, sister?

SECOND WITCH
Killing swine.

THIRD WITCH
Sister, where thou?

FIRST WITCH
A sailor's wife had chestnuts in her lap,
And mounched, and mounched, and mounched.
5   "Give me," quoth I.

---

54 *Bellona* in Roman mythology, the sister of the God of War, Mars.
61 *Saint Colme's Inch* St. Columba's Island, Inchcolm in the Firth of Forth, near Edinburgh.

The King of Norway himself, leading terrifying numbers
   of men,
and assisted by that most disloyal traitor,
the Thane of Cawdor, began a menacing battle;
until the war goddess's bridegroom (i.e., Macbeth), dressed in
   well-tried armor,
55   met him face to face and parried each of his movements,
sword against sword, rebellious arm against arm,
checking his overconfidence, and, to conclude,
the victory was ours.

KING
Very fortunate for us!

ROSS
Now
Sweno, the King of Norway, desires a peace treaty,
60   but we would not permit him to bury his men
until he had paid, at Saint Colme's Island,
ten thousand dollars as a ransom.

KING
The Thane of Cawdor will no longer fool me
in matters that concern me deeply. Go and announce his
   immediate execution
65   and greet Macbeth as the new Thane of Cawdor.

ROSS
I'll see that it's done.

KING
What Cawdor has lost, noble Macbeth has won.
    They exit.

Act I, Scene iii: A heath. Thunder. Enter the Three Witches.

FIRST WITCH
Where have you been, sister?

SECOND WITCH
Killing pigs.

THIRD WITCH
And sister, where have you been?

FIRST WITCH
A sailor's wife had hot chestnuts in her lap,
and chewed, and chewed, and chewed.
5   "Give me some," I asked.

---

62 *dollars* English for the German *Thaler,* a silver coin well known
to the Elizabethans. It is an anachronism here, since the coin was first minted
in the sixteenth century and *Macbeth* takes place in the eleventh century.

"Aroint thee, witch!" the rump-fed ronyon* cries.
Her husband's to Aleppo gone, master o' th' Tiger:*
But in a sieve I'll thither sail,
And, like a rat without a tail,
10   I'll do, I'll do, and I'll do.
SECOND WITCH
    I'll give thee a wind.
FIRST WITCH
    Th' art kind.
THIRD WITCH
    And I another.
FIRST WITCH
    I myself have all the other;
15   And the very ports they blow,
    All the quarters that they know
    I' th' shipman's card.
    I'll drain him dry as hay:
    Sleep shall neither night nor day
20   Hang upon his penthouse lid;
    He shall live a man forbid:
    Weary sev'nights nine times nine
    Shall he dwindle, peak, and pine:
    Though his bark cannot be lost,
25   Yet it shall be tempest-tossed.
    Look what I have.
SECOND WITCH
    Show me, show me.
FIRST WITCH
    Here I have a pilot's thumb,
    Wracked as homeward he did come.
            Drum within.
THIRD WITCH
30   A drum, a drum!
    Macbeth doth come.
ALL
    The Weird* Sisters, hand in hand,
    Posters of the sea and land,
    Thus do go about, about:

---

    6 *ronyon* a mangy or scabby creature, but usually used as a general
term of contempt.
    7 *Tiger* the name of the ship making the journey to Aleppo, a city in
northern Syria.

"Get away from me, you witch!" the fat-bottomed bitch cries.
Her husband, the skipper of the *Tiger*, has sailed to Aleppo,
but I'll sail there myself in a sieve
and, like a rat without a tail,
10 I'll do all sorts of mischief to him. I will, I will, I will!

SECOND WITCH
I'll give you a good wind for sailing.

FIRST WITCH
You are kind.

THIRD WITCH
And I'll give you another good wind.

FIRST WITCH
I have control of all the other winds,
15 and I have control of the seaports they blow toward
and the places they blow from;
in fact, all the points of the sailor's compass.
I'll drain the skipper's blood until his body is dry as hay.
Neither by night nor day will sleep
20 weigh down his eyelids.
He shall live like a cursed man.
For eighty-one weary weeks
he shall shrink, fade, and waste away.
Though his ship cannot be sunk,
25 I'll see to it that storms continue to toss it about.
Look what I have here.

SECOND WITCH
Show me, show me.

FIRST WITCH
Here, I have the thumb of a ship's pilot,
who was shipwrecked on his homeward voyage.
A drum is heard from offstage.

THIRD WITCH
30 A drum, A drum!
Macbeth is coming.

ALL (*joining hands and dancing around a kettle*)
The Weird Sisters, hand in hand,
swift travelers over sea and land,
thus do dance around, around:

---

32   *weird* from the Old English "wyrd" meaning fate or, in the plural,
"the Fates," or Parcae (in Roman mythology the three goddesses supposed
to control the course of human life).

35   Thrice to thine, and thrice to mine,
        And thrice again, to make up nine.
        Peace! The charm's wound up.

            Enter MACBETH *and* BANQUO.

MACBETH
        So foul and fair a day I have not seen.

BANQUO
        How far is 't called to Forres?* What are these
40   So withered, and so wild in their attire,
        That look not like th' inhabitants o' th' earth
        And yet are on 't? Live you, or are you aught
        That man may question? You seem to understand me,
        By each at once her choppy finger laying
45   Upon her skinny lips. You should be women,
        And yet your beards forbid me to interpret
        That you are so.

MACBETH
                            Speak, if you can: what are you?

FIRST WITCH
        All hail, Macbeth! Hail to thee, Thane of Glamis!*

SECOND WITCH
        All hail, Macbeth! Hail to thee, Thane of Cawdor!*

THIRD WITCH
50   All hail, Macbeth, that shalt be King hereafter!

BANQUO
        Good sir, why do you start, and seem to fear
        Things that do sound so fair? I' th' name of truth,
        Are ye fantastical, or that indeed
        Which outwardly ye show? My noble partner
55   You greet with present grace and great prediction
        Of noble having and of royal hope,
        That he seems rapt withal: to me you speak not.
        If you can look into the seeds of time,
        And say which grain will grow and which will not,
60   Speak then to me, who neither beg nor fear
        Your favors nor your hate.

FIRST WITCH
        Hail!

---

39 *Forres* a town in northern Scotland, to the south of Moray Firth,
between Elgin and Nairn.
48 *Glamis* a castle and village north of Dundee, near the modern town
of Forfar. Most editors agree that Shakespeare pronounced the word in

35 three times for the first sister, three for the second,
and three for the third, to make up nine.
Hush! The charm's all set to work.

      Enter MACBETH *and* BANQUO.

MACBETH

I have never seen a day so clear and yet so overcast.

BANQUO

How far is it to the town of Forres?—What sort of creatures
are these

40 that are so shriveled up and so wildly dressed?
They don't look like persons who live on the earth
and yet they are on it nevertheless. Are you alive and are you
creatures
that a man can talk to? You seem to understand me
because each of you signals to me by putting a chapped finger

45 to her skinny lips. You must be women,
and yet your beards prevent me from thinking
that you really are.

MACBETH

Speak, if you can : what are you?

FIRST WITCH

All hail, Macbeth! Hail to thee, Thane of Glamis!

SECOND WITCH

All hail, Macbeth! Hail to thee, Thane of Cawdor!

THIRD WITCH

50 All hail, Macbeth, who will soon be King.

BANQUO (*to Macbeth*)

Good sir, why are you startled and seem to fear
predictions that sound so favorable? (*To the Witches*)
    Truthfully,
are you a figment of our imagination or are you

55 what you seem to be? My noble partner, Macbeth,
you greet with his present title and lofty predictions
of future nobility and with the hope of becoming King.
He seems to be carried away by it all. You say nothing to me.
If you can look into the seeds of time,
and foretell which grain will grow and which will not,

60 then speak to me, who neither seeks nor fears
your favors or your hate.

FIRST WITCH

Hail!

---

two syllables.
   49   *Cawdor*   located in northwestern Nairnshire, between Inverness and
Forres.

SECOND WITCH
  Hail!
THIRD WITCH
  Hail!
FIRST WITCH
65 Lesser than Macbeth, and greater.
SECOND WITCH
  Not so happy, yet much happier.
THIRD WITCH
  Thou shalt get kings, though thou be none.
  So all hail, Macbeth and Banquo!
FIRST WITCH
  Banquo and Macbeth, all hail!
MACBETH
70 Stay, you imperfect speakers, tell me more:
  By Sinel's death I know I am Thane of Glamis;
  But how of Cawdor? The Thane of Cawdor lives,
  A prosperous gentleman; and to be King
  Stands not within the prospect of belief,
75 No more than to be Cawdor. Say from whence
  You owe this strange intelligence? Or why
  Upon this blasted heath you stop our way
  With such prophetic greeting? Speak, I charge you.
      Witches vanish.
BANQUO
  The earth hath bubbles as the water has,
80 And these are of them. Whether are they vanished?
MACBETH
  Into the air, and what seemed corporal melted
  As breath into the wind. Would they had stayed!
BANQUO
  Were such things here as we do speak about?
  Or have we eaten on the insane root*
85 That takes the reason prisoner?
MACBETH
  Your children shall be kings.
BANQUO
                    You shall be King.

---

84 *insane root* a herb or root causing insanity. Shakespeare may have had in mind such plants as hemlock, henbane, or deadly nightshade.

SECOND WITCH
   Hail!
THIRD WITCH
   Hail!
FIRST WITCH
65   You will be lesser than Macbeth and greater.
SECOND WITCH
   You will not be so fortunate and yet you will be much more
      fortunate.
THIRD WITCH
   You will give birth to kings although you will never be one
      yourself.
   So all hail, Macbeth and Banquo!
FIRST WITCH
   Banquo and Macbeth, all hail!
MACBETH
70   Wait, you speakers of half-truths; tell me more.
   By the death of my father, Sinel, I know I am Thane of Glamis,
   but how can I be Thane of Cawdor, since Cawdor still lives,
   a thriving gentleman? And the possibility of my becoming King
   is as unbelievable
75   as my becoming Thane of Cawdor. Tell me where
   you got this startling information, and why
   you have stopped us on this barren heath
   with such a prophetic greeting. I order you to speak.
      The Witches vanish.
BANQUO
   The earth has bubbles as water does,
80   and these witches are just as insubstantial. Where did they
      vanish to?
MACBETH
   Into the air, and what seemed to be bodies melted
   like breath in the wind. I wish they had stayed.
BANQUO
   Were these creatures that we're talking about really here?
   Or have we eaten the root that causes insanity
85   and makes human reason a prisoner?
MACBETH
   Your children shall be kings.
BANQUO
   But you shall be King.

MACBETH
And Thane of Cawdor too. Went it not so?
BANQUO
To th' selfsame tune and words .Who's here?
                Enter ROSS *and* ANGUS.
ROSS
The King hath happily received, Macbeth,
90 The news of thy success; and when he reads
Thy personal venture in the rebels' fight,
His wonders and his praises do contend
Which should be thine or his. Silenced with that,
In viewing o'er the rest o' th' selfsame day,
95 He finds thee in the stout Norweyan ranks,
Nothing afeard of what thyself didst make,
Strange images of death. As thick as hail
Came post with post, and every one did bear
Thy praises in his kingdom's great defense,
And poured them down before him.
ANGUS
100   We are sent
To give thee, from our royal master, thanks;
Only to herald thee into his sight,
Not pay thee.
ROSS
And for an earnest of a greater honor,
105 He bade me, from him, call thee Thane of Cawdor;
In which addition, hail, most worthy thane!
For it is thine.
BANQUO
                    What, can the devil speak true?
MACBETH
The Thane of Cawdor lives: why do you dress me
In borrowed robes?
ANGUS
                    Who was the thane lives yet,
110 But under heavy judgment bears that life
Which he deserves to lose. Whether he was combined
With those of Norway, or did line the rebel
With hidden help and vantage, or that with both

MACBETH
And Thane of Cawdor too. Isn't that how it went?
BANQUO
That's the very tune and lyrics. Who's here?
Enter ROSS *and* ANGUS.
ROSS
Macbeth, the King has joyfully heard
90 the news of your success, and when he considers
your own personal danger in the fight with the rebels,
he's caught between the impulse to wonder at your deeds and
the desire to praise you—
and he can't decide which to do. Left speechless,
and looking back over the rest of that day of battle,
95 he also finds that you were in the midst of the fight against the
strong Norwegian troops,
fearless of what you yourself created—
grotesque visions of death. As thick as hail
came messenger after messenger, each carrying
reports praising your great defense of the kingdom,
and they heaped these reports before the King.
ANGUS
100 We were sent
from the King to thank you.
We've only come to bring you to the King;
it's not for us to reward you.
ROSS
And as a pledge of a greater honor
105 the King has directed me to address you as Thane of Cawdor;
by which title, then, greetings, most worthy thane!
The title is yours.
BANQUO
What, can the devil speak the truth?
MACBETH
The Thane of Cawdor lives. Why do you dress me
in robes that don't belong to me?
ANGUS
He who was the thane still lives,
110 but he now lives under sentence of death,
a judgment he well deserves. Whether he was allied
with the Norwegian forces, or supported the rebel troops
with secret aid and assistance, or with both parties

He labored in his country's wrack, I know not;
115 But treasons capital, confessed and proved,
Have overthrown him.

MACBETH [*Aside*]
                        Glamis, and Thane of Cawdor:
The greatest is behind. [*To* ROSS *and* ANGUS] Thanks for your
    pains.
[*Aside to* BANQUO] Do you not hope your children shall be kings,
When those that gave the Thane of Cawdor to me
Promised no less to them?

BANQUO [*Aside to* MACBETH]
120   That, trusted home,
Might yet enkindle you unto the crown,
Besides the Thane of Cawdor. But 'tis strange:
And oftentimes, to win us to our harm,
The instruments of darkness tell us truths,
125 Win us with honest trifles, to betray 's
In deepest consequence.
Cousins, a word, I pray you.

MACBETH [*Aside*]
                           Two truths are told,
As happy prologues to the swelling act
Of the imperial theme.—I thank you, gentlemen.—
130 [*Aside*] This supernatural soliciting
Cannot be ill, cannot be good. If ill,
Why hath it given me earnest of success,
Commencing in a truth? I am Thane of Cawdor:
If good, why do I yield to that suggestion
135 Whose horrid image doth unfix my hair
And make my seated heart knock at my ribs,
Against the use of nature? Present fears
Are less than horrible imaginings.
My thought, whose murder yet is but fantastical,
140 Shakes so my single state of man that function
Is smothered in surmise, and nothing is
But what is not.

BANQUO
                Look, how our partner's rapt.

conspired to ruin his country, I don't know;
115 but high treason, confessed and proved,
has ruined him.
MACBETH (*to himself*)
Glamis, and Thane of Cawdor—
the greatest prophecy is yet to come.
(*To Ross and Angus*) Thanks for your troubles.
(*To Banquo*) Don't you hope your children will be kings,
since those witches who promised the Thane of Cawdor to
me also
promised no less to your sons?
BANQUO (*to Macbeth*)
120 That prophecy, fulfilled,
might yet incite you to seek the crown
in addition to being Thane of Cawdor. But it is strange
how often, to trap us into danger,
the devil's workers use truths,
125 win us over with half-truths, only to trick us
in the important final outcome.
(*To Ross and Angus*) Kinsmen, I wish to have a word with you.
MACBETH (*to himself*)
Two of the prophecies have proven true
and serve as a fortunate beginning to the inevitable movement
by which I become king. (*To Ross and Angus*) I thank you,
gentlemen.
130 (*To himself*) This supernatural attempt to influence me
can neither be good nor bad. If it were bad,
why has it given me a promise of success
by beginning with a truth? I am Thane of Cawdor.
If it were good, why am I giving in to that temptation (i.e., to
kill Duncan),
135 whose horrible vision makes my hair stand on end
and causes my steadfast heart to beat wildly against my ribs
in a most unnatural way? My real fears
are less troublesome than my horrible fantasies.
My murderous thoughts, which are still only imaginary,
140 shake me up so violently that my normal powers
are smothered by these speculations and nothing seems real
except what hasn't happened yet.
BANQUO (*to Ross and Angus*)
Look, how my partner is lost in thought.

MACBETH [*Aside*]
  If chance will have me King, why, chance may crown me,
  Without my stir.

BANQUO
                  New honors come upon him,
145   Like our strange garments, cleave not to their mold
  But with the aid of use.

MACBETH [*Aside*]
                  Come what come may,
  Time and the hour runs through the roughest day.

BANQUO
  Worthy Macbeth, we stay upon your leisure.

MACBETH
  Give me your favor. My dull brain was wrought
150   With things forgotten. Kind gentlemen, your pains
  Are registered where every day I turn
  The leaf to read them. Let us toward the King.
  [*Aside to* BANQUO] Think upon what hath chanced, and at
      more time,
  The interim having weighted it, let us speak
  Our free hearts each to other.

BANQUO
155   Very gladly.

MACBETH
  Till then, enough. Come, friends.
      Exeunt.

Scene iv: [*Forres. The castle.*] *Flourish. Enter King* [DUNCAN],
LENNOX, MALCOLM, DONALBAIN, *and Attendants.*

KING
  Is execution done on Cawdor? Are not
  Those in commission yet returned?

MALCOLM
                  My liege,
  They are not yet come back. But I have spoke

MACBETH (*to himself*)

    If chance intends to make me king, why

    chance may give me the crown

    without my doing anything at all in my own behalf.

BANQUO (*to Ross and Angus*)

    New honors hang on Macbeth

145   like new clothes : they don't fit the body

    until they have been worn a while.

MACBETH (*to himself*)

    Whatever may come,

    time and tide continue through the roughest day (and bring a

        solution to every difficulty).

BANQUO (*to Macbeth*)

    Worthy Macbeth, we are waiting for you.

MACBETH

    I beg your pardon. My dull brain was busy

150   with things of the past. Kind gentlemen, your efforts on my

        behalf

    are written in the book of my memory where every day I

        will turn

    the page to read them. Let us start on our way to the King.

    (*To Banquo*) Think about what has happened and when we

        have more time—

    having meanwhile considered the matter carefully—let us speak

    openly about our thoughts and feelings.

BANQUO

155   Very gladly.

MACBETH

    Until then that's enough said. Come, friends.

        They exit.

Act I, Scene iv: A room in the castle at Forres. Trumpets are sounded. Enter KING DUNCAN and his sons, MALCOLM and DONALBAIN. They are accompanied by LENNOX and Attendants.

KING

    Has the Thane of Cawdor been executed? Haven't

    the officials charged with the execution returned yet?

MALCOLM

    My lord,

    they have not yet returned, but I spoke

With one that saw him die, who did report
5   That very frankly he confessed his treasons,
Implored your Highness' pardon and set forth
A deep repentance: nothing in his life
Became him like the leaving it. He died
As one that had been studied in his death,
10   To throw away the dearest thing he owed
As 'twere a careless trifle.

KING
There's no art
To find the mind's construction in the face:
He was a gentleman on whom I built
An absolute trust.
Enter MACBETH, BANQUO, ROSS, *and* ANGUS.
O worthiest cousin!
15   The sin of my ingratitude even now
Was heavy on me: thou art so far before,
That swiftest wing of recompense is slow
To overtake thee. Would thou hadst less deserved,
That the proportion both of thanks and payment
20   Might have been mine! Only I have left to say,
More is thy due than more than all can pay.

MACBETH
The service and the loyalty I owe,
In doing it, pays itself. Your Highness' part
Is to receive our duties: and our duties
25   Are to your throne and state children and servants;
Which do but what they should, by doing every thing
Safe toward your love and honor.

KING
Welcome hither.
I have begun to plant thee, and will labor
To make thee full of growing. Noble Banquo,
30   That hast no less deserved, nor must be known
No less to have done so, let me enfold thee
And hold thee to my heart.

5   with someone who saw Cawdor die. He reported
    that the thane frankly confessed his treasons,
    begged your Highness' pardon, and expressed
    a deep repentance. He did nothing in his life
    more fitting than the way he left it. He died
    as if he had rehearsed his own death,

10 appearing to throw away the dearest thing he owned (i.e., his
        life)
    as if it were a worthless trifle.

KING
    There's no way
    to read someone's character from studying his face.
    Cawdor was a gentleman in whom
    I had absolute faith.
            Enter MACBETH, BANQUO, ROSS, *and* ANGUS.
    (*To Macbeth*) O most worthy kinsman!

15 The sin of my ingratitude to you still
    weighs on my mind. You have succeeded so preeminently
    that the swiftest flight of reward is too slow
    to catch up with you. I wish you had deserved less,
    so that I might have been able to give you thanks and payment

20 in a proportion greater than you deserve. I can only say
    that more is owing to you than can ever be repaid.

MACBETH
    Being of service and the loyalty I owe you
    are their own reward. Your Highness' role
    is to accept the duties of his loyal subjects, and our duties

25 are to your throne and country like those of children and
        servants,
    who only do what they should by doing all
    they can to safeguard your well-being with love and honor.

KING
    You are welcome here.
    I have begun to concern myself with you, and I'll work
    to make you thrive. (*To Banquo*) Noble Banquo,

30 you are no less deserving than Macbeth and your deeds must
        be recognized
    as much as his. Let me embrace you
    and hold you close to my heart.

BANQUO
                        There if I grow,
The harvest is your own.

KING
                        My plenteous joys,
Wanton in fullness, seek to hide themselves
In drops of sorrow. Sons, kinsmen, thanes,
And you whose places are the nearest, know,
We will establish our estate upon
Our eldest, Malcolm, whom we name hereafter
The Prince of Cumberland;* which honor must
Not unaccompanied invest him only,
But signs of nobleness, like stars, shall shine
On all deservers. From hence to Inverness,*
And bind us further to you.

MACBETH
The rest is labor, which is not used for you.
I'll be myself the harbinger, and make joyful
The hearing of my wife with your approach;
So, humbly take my leave.

KING
                        My worthy Cawdor!

MACBETH   [*Aside*]
The Prince of Cumberland! That is a step
On which I must fall down, or else o'erleap,
For in my way it lies. Stars, hide your fires;
Let not light see my black and deep desires!
The eye wink at the hand; yet let that be
Which the eye fears, when it is done, to see.
            Exit.

KING
True, worthy Banquo; he is full so valiant,
And in his commendations I am fed;
It is a banquet to me. Let's after him,
Whose care is gone before to bid us welcome.
It is a peerless kinsman.
            Flourish. Exeunt.

---

39   *Prince of Cumberland*   At the time of Duncan's reign the throne of
Scotland was not hereditary. If the King's successor was designated during the
monarch's lifetime, he received the title of Prince of Cumberland, as a sign

BANQUO
  If I grow there,
  the harvest belongs to you.
KING
  My many joys,
  overflowing in fullness, are trying to hide themselves
35 in (what might look like) tears of sorrow. (*To the court*) Sons,
    relatives, thanes,
  and you whose ranks are nearest to the throne, I here proclaim
  that I will bequeath my kingdom to
  my eldest son, Malcolm, and to him I give the title
  Prince of Cumberland. This honor bestowed on him
40 shall not be the only one given,
  but noble titles shall shine like stars
  on all who deserve them. (*To Macbeth*) Let us go to Inverness
    Castle
  and strengthen our friendship further.
MACBETH
  All other labor is tedious which is not done in the service of the
    King.
45 I myself will be the messenger and will carry the joyful news
  of your visit to my wife.
  Thus (*with a gesture of parting*) I humbly take my leave of you.
KING
  My worthy Cawdor!

MACBETH (*to himself*)
  The Prince of Cumberland! That is a step
  that will trip me up, or else I must leap over it,
50 because it lies in my way. Stars, hide your fiery light.
  Don't let any light shine on my black and deep desires.
  Don't let the eye see what the hand is doing; yet let that deed
    be done
  which the eye fears to look at after it has been done.
      He exits.
KING (*to Banquo*)
  It's true, worthy Banquo, Macbeth is very brave
55 and I feed on compliments to him;
  such praise is a banquet to me. Let's follow him,
  who has so considerately gone before us to prepare our welcome.
  He is a kinsman without any equal.
      The trumpets sound and they exit.

---

of his future succession.
  42 *Inverness* a Scottish town. Specifically the reference is to Macbeth's
castle there. This is the first indication that Duncan intends to visit Macbeth.

Scene v: [Inverness. MACBETH's *castle.] Enter* MACBETH's *wife alone, with a letter.*

LADY MACBETH [*Reads*]
"They met me in the day of success; and I have learned by the perfect'st report they have more in them than mortal knowl-edge. When I burned in desire to question them further, they made themselves air, into which they vanished. Whiles I stood
5   rapt in the wonder of it, came missives from the King, who all-hailed me 'Thane of Cawdor'; by which title, before, these Weird Sisters saluted me, and referred me to the coming on of time, with 'Hail, King that shalt be!' This have I thought good to de-liver thee, my dearest partner of greatness, that thou mightst not
10   lose the dues of rejoicing, by being ignorant of what greatness is promised thee. Lay it to thy heart, and farewell."
Glamis thou art, and Cawdor, and shalt be
What thou art promised. Yet do I fear thy nature;
It is too full o' th' milk of human kindness
15   To catch the nearest way. Thou wouldst be great,
Art not without ambition, but without
The illness* should attend it. What thou wouldst highly,
That wouldst thou holily; wouldst not play false,
And yet wouldst wrongly win. Thou'dst have, great Glamis,
20   That which cries, "Thus thou must do," if thou have it;
And that which rather thou dost fear to do
Than wishest should be undone. Hie thee hither,
That I may pour my spirits in thine ear,
And chastise with the valor of my tongue
25   All that impedes thee from the golden round
Which fate and metaphysical aid doth seem

---

17   *illness*   the evil quality—ruthlessness—which should go along with ambition.

Act I, Scene v: Macbeth's castle in Inverness. LADY MACBETH
enters, reading a letter from her husband.

LADY MACBETH

"The Witches met me on the day of our victory, and I have
learned from the
most reliable source that they have knowledge beyond that of
mortal men.
When I burned with desire to question them further, they
made themselves invisible and vanished into thin air. While I
stood

5   dazed at the wonder of it, messengers came from the King who
greeted me as 'Thane of Cawdor,' the title by which the Weird
Sisters had previously greeted me. The Witches also had me look
to the future
with their cry, 'Hail, King that shall be!' I thought it best to
send this news to you, my dearest partner in greatness, in order
that you might not

10   be deprived of the rejoicing to which you are entitled by being
ignorant of the greatness that is
promised you. Give it your deepest thought, and farewell."
You are already Thane of Glamis and Thane of Cawdor,
and you will be King as you were promised. Yet I fear your
nature;
it is too full of the milk of human kindness

15   to take the easiest path to success. You would like to be great
and are not without ambition, but you lack
the ruthlessness that should go with it. The high aspirations
you have
you wish to achieve in a holy manner. You don't want to play
falsely
and yet you want to win dishonestly. Great Glamis, you want

20   that (i.e., the crown) which cries you must do something
(i.e., kill Duncan) to get it.
You'd prefer to be afraid to murder Duncan rather
than once having done it, regret the deed. Hurry up and come
here
so that I can pour my strong spirits into your ear,
and, with the strength of my words, reprimand

25   all that prevents you from gaining the golden crown
with which fate and supernatural help seem

To have thee crowned withal.
    Enter Messenger.

                      What is your tidings?

MESSENGER
The King comes here tonight.
LADY MACBETH
                      Thou'rt mad to say it!
Is not thy master with him, who, were 't so,
30   Would have informed for preparation?
MESSENGER
So please you, it is true. Our thane is coming.
One of my fellows had the speed of him,
Who, almost dead for breath, had scarcely more
Than would make up his message.
LADY MACBETH
                    Give him tending;
He brings great news.
    Exit Messenger.
35   The raven* himself is hoarse
That croaks the fatal entrance of Duncan
Under my battlements. Come, you spirits
That tend on mortal thoughts, unsex* me here,
And fill me, from the crown to the toe, top-full
40   Of direct cruelty! Make thick my blood,
Stop up th' access and passage to remorse,
That no compunctious visitings of nature
Shake my fell purpose, nor keep peace between
Th' effect and it! Come to my woman's breasts,
45   And take my milk for gall, you murd'ring ministers,
Wherever in your sightless substances
You wait on nature's mischief! Come, thick night,
And pall thee in the dunnest smoke of hell,
That my keen knife see not the wound it makes,
50   Nor heaven peep through the blanket of the dark,
To cry "Hold, hold!"
    Enter MACBETH.
                Great Glamis! Worthy Cawdor!
Greater than both, by the all-hail hereafter!

---

35 *raven* a bird of ill-omen and fateful powers. Edgar Allen Poe, for example, makes just such use of the bird in his poem "The Raven."

already to have crowned you.
> *Enter a Messenger.*

What is your news?

MESSENGER
> The King is coming here tonight.

LADY MACBETH
> You're crazy to say such a thing!
> Isn't your master with the King, who, if it were true,
> would have informed me, so that preparations could be made?

MESSENGER
> I beg your pardon, but it is true. Our thane Macbeth is coming.
> One of my fellow servants outrode him
> and was so out of breath, he scarcely had
> enough left to speak the message.

LADY MACBETH
> Give the rider all necessary attention;
> he brings great news.
> *Exit Messenger.*
>
> The raven itself is hoarse
> from croaking news of Duncan's fatal entrance
> under my roof. Come, you spirits
> that have charge of murderous thoughts, unsex me here,
> and fill me, from the crown of my head to my toes, completely full
> of horrible cruelty! Thicken my blood,
> stop up all passages that could give pity an entrance,
> so that no natural feelings of compassion
> can weaken my cruel purpose, nor come between
> the actual murder and my willing it! Come to my woman's
>   breasts
> and replace my milk with bitter bile, you murderous agents—
> come from wherever it is you wait in your invisibility
> ready to help abuse nature's laws! Come, thick night,
> and wrap yourself in the darkest smoke of hell,
> so that my sharp knife cannot see the wound it makes,
> nor heaven peep through the blanket of darkness
> to cry, "Stop, stop!"
> *Enter MACBETH.*
>
> Great Thane of Glamis! Worthy Thane of Cawdor!
> and according to the witches' prophecies, destined to be greater
>   than both.

30

35

40

45

50

---

38 *unsex* Lady Macbeth is asking to be free of mercy and gentleness, qualities traditionally associated with the female sex.

Thy letters have transported me beyond
This ignorant present, and I feel now
The future in the instant.

MACBETH

55   My dearest love,
Duncan comes here tonight.

LADY MACBETH

                              And when goes hence?

MACBETH

Tomorrow, as he purposes.

LADY MACBETH

                              O, never
Shall sun that morrow see!
Your face, my thane, is as a book where men
60   May read strange matters. To beguile the time,
Look like the time; bear welcome in your eye,
Your hand, your tongue: look like th' innocent flower,
But be the serpent under 't. He that's coming
Must be provided for: and you shall put
65   This night's great business into my dispatch;
Which shall to all our nights and days to come
Give solely sovereign sway and masterdom.

MACBETH

We will speak further.

LADY MACBETH

                              Only look up clear.
To alter favor ever is to fear.
70   Leave all the rest to me.
          Exeunt.

Scene vi: [*Before* MACBETH's *castle.*] *Hautboys and torches. Enter King* [DUNCAN], MALCOLM, BANQUO, LENNOX, MACDUFF, ROSS, ANGUS, *and Attendants.*

KING

This castle hath a pleasant seat; the air
Nimbly and sweetly recommends itself
Unto our gentle senses.

Your letter has carried me beyond
this uncertain present, and I feel that
the future is in the here and now.

MACBETH
55   My dearest love,
Duncan comes here tonight.

LADY MACBETH
And when will he leave?

MACBETH
He plans to leave tomorrow.

LADY MACBETH
The sun shall never see that day.
Your face, my lord, is like an open book where one
60   can read strange things. To deceive the world,
behave as other people do. Welcome him with your eye,
your handshake, your conversation. Look like the innocent flower
but be the serpent hidden underneath it. For Duncan's coming,
preparations must be made, and you must put
65   this night's important business under my direction.
It is a business which will give us control and supremacy
for the rest of our nights and days.

MACBETH
We will speak further about it.

LADY MACBETH
Just look innocent—
a troubled face is always dangerous.
70   Leave all the rest to me.
       They exit.

*Act I, Scene vi: In front of Inverness Castle. Music of oboes is
heard and lighted torches are brought on stage.* KING DUNCAN
enters, accompanied by MALCOLM, DONALBAIN, BANQUO,
LENNOX, MACDUFF, ROSS, ANGUS, *and Attendants.*

KING
This castle has a pleasant setting. The air
briskly and sweetly appeals
to our senses and soothes them.

BANQUO
                          This guest of summer,
      The temple-haunting martlet,* does approve
5   By his loved mansionry that the heaven's breath
      Smells wooingly here. No jutty, frieze,
      Buttress, nor coign of vantage, but this bird
      Hath made his pendent bed and procreant cradle.
      Where they most breed and haunt, I have observed
      The air is delicate.
                  Enter LADY [MACBETH].
KING
10   See, see, our honored hostess!
      The love that follows us sometime is our trouble,
      Which still we thank as love.* Herein I teach you
      How you shall bid God 'ild us for your pains
      And thank us for your trouble.
LADY MACBETH
                                All our service
15   In every point twice done, and then done double,
      Were poor and single business to contend
      Against those honors deep and broad wherewith
      Your Majesty loads our house. For those of old,
      And the late dignities heaped up to them,
      We rest your hermits.
KING
20   Where's the Thane of Cawdor?
      We coursed him at the heels, and had a purpose
      To be his purveyor: but he rides well,
      And his great love, sharp as his spur, hath holp him
      To his home before us. Fair and noble hostess,
      We are your guest tonight.
LADY MACBETH
25   Your servants ever
      Have theirs, themselves, and what is theirs, in compt,
      To make their audit at your Highness' pleasure,
      Still to return your own.
KING
                          Give me your hand.

---

      4 *martlet* the house martin, a small European bird of the swallow family.
      12 *love* In this instance, Duncan is speaking of the love of a subject
for his monarch, that is, loyalty, a sense of duty to one's feudal lord.

BANQUO
This summer guest,
the little martlet that likes to live near churches, proves
5   by his beloved nest that the air of heaven
smells tempting here. There is no projection, trim,
support, or convenient corner of the castle where this bird
has not found a place for his hanging bed and breeding nest.
I have observed that wherever these birds breed and flock
the air is especially fine.
Enter LADY MACBETH.

KING
10   See, see, our honored hostess!
The love that pursues me sometimes also troubles me,
but still I am grateful for this love. In this way I teach you
how to ask God to reward me for the trouble you take
and thank me for being a nuisance to you.

LADY MACBETH
All our service for you,
15   even if we doubled it and then doubled it again,
would be a poor and feeble effort compared
with the deep and broad honors
your Majesty bestows upon our house. For the past honors
and the dignities recently added to them,
we remain your servants who will always pray for you.

KING
20   Where's the Thane of Cawdor?
I pursued him closely, intending
to get here before him. But Macbeth rides well,
and his great love for you—sharp as his spur—helped him
to get home before me. Fair and noble hostess,
I am your guest tonight.

LADY MACBETH
25   Your servants always
have their whole household, themselves, and their possessions
  itemized
and ready to be accounted for at your Highness' pleasure. We are
always ready to return to you what is already yours.

KING
Give me your hand.

Conduct me to mine host: we love him highly,
30   And shall continue our graces towards him.
By your leave, hostess.
        Exeunt.

Scene vii: [MACBETH's *castle.*] *Hautboys. Torches. Enter a Sewer, and divers Servants with dishes and service over the stage. Then enter* MACBETH.

MACBETH
If it were done when 'tis done, then 'twere well
It were done quickly. If th' assassination
Could trammel up the consequence, and catch,
With his surcease, success; that but this blow
5   Might be the be-all and the end-all—here,
But here, upon this bank and shoal of time,
We'd jump the life to come. But in these cases
We still have judgment here; that we but teach
Bloody instructions, which, being taught, return
10   To plague th' inventor: this even-handed justice
Commends th' ingredients of our poisoned chalice
To our own lips. He's here in double trust:
First, as I am his kinsman and his subject,
Strong both against the deed; then, as his host,
15   Who should against his murderer shut the door,
Not bear the knife myself. Besides, this Duncan
Hath borne his faculties so meek, hath been
So clear in his great office, that his virtues
Will plead like angels trumpet-tongued against
20   The deep damnation of his taking-off;
And pity, like a naked newborn babe,
Striding the blast, or heaven's cherubin horsed
Upon the sightless couriers of the air,
Shall blow the horrid deed in every eye,
25   That tears shall drown the wind. I have no spur

Lead me to my host. I love him greatly,
30   and will continue to show him favor.
With your permission, hostess, (I will enter your castle).
    They exit.

Act I, Scene vii: A room near the banqueting hall of Macbeth's castle. Oboes are playing and the torches are lit. The supper for KING DUNCAN *is in progress and the chief butler and other servants cross the stage with platters of food, etc.* MACBETH *has left the banqueting hall to be alone with his thoughts.*

MACBETH
If it were over and done with once it is done, then it is best
to do it quickly. If the murder itself
could cut off any troubling consequences and attain a final
        success
with Duncan's death; if, by striking this blow only,
5   all plans would be accomplished and there would be no
        aftermath—
here, right here and now, in this one small moment of time—
I'd risk my chances of salvation in the hereafter. But in cases
        like these,
we always have earthly judgment in this life; thus we only
        teach
bloody ways of doing things, which once taught return
10   to pursue the teacher. This impartial justice
offers us the contents of our own poisoned cup
for us to drink. Besides, Duncan doubly trusts us:
first, I am his kinsman and his loyal subject,
both strong persuasions against the deed. Then, I am his host,
15   who should lock the door against his murderer
rather than carry the knife myself. Moreover, Duncan
has used his kingly power so gently and has been
so upright in his high office, that his virtues
will plead like angels with tongues of trumpets against
20   the damnable infamy of his murder.
And pity—like a naked newborn baby
riding the wind, or like a troop of heavenly angels
astride the invisible steeds of the air—
shall blow the frightful deed into every eye,
25   so that compassionate tears shall drown the wind. I have no spurs

To prick the sides of my intent, but only
Vaulting ambition, which o'erleaps itself
And falls on th' other side.
                Enter LADY [MACBETH].
                                How now? What news?
LADY MACBETH
    He has almost supped. Why have you left the chamber?
MACBETH
    Hath he asked for me?
LADY MACBETH
30   Know you not he has?
MACBETH
    We will proceed no further in this business:
    He hath honored me of late, and I have bought
    Golden opinions from all sorts of people,
    Which would be worn now in their newest gloss,
    Not cast aside so soon.
LADY MACBETH
35   Was the hope drunk
    Wherein you dressed yourself? Hath it slept since?
    And wakes it now, to look so green and pale
    At what it did so freely? From this time
    Such I account thy love. Art thou afeard
40 To be the same in thine own act and valor
    As thou art in desire? Wouldst thou have that
    Which thou esteem'st the ornament of life,
    And live a coward in thine own esteem,
    Letting "I dare not" wait upon "I would,"
    Like the poor cat i' th' adage?*
MACBETH
45   Prithee, peace!
    I dare do all that may become a man;
    Who dares do more is none.
LADY MACBETH
                                What beast was 't then
    That made you break this enterprise to me?
    When you durst do it, then you were a man;
50 And to be more than what you were, you would

---

44 *poor cat i' the adage* a familiar saying about a cat that wanted fish,
but was unwilling to wet her feet to catch them.

to prick my purpose, like a horse, into action, but only
my boundless ambition, which leaps over the horse and falls
on the other side.
    Enter LADY MACBETH.
How is everything going? What's the news?

LADY MACBETH

The King has almost finished supper. Why did you leave the
    banqueting room?

MACBETH

Did he ask for me?

LADY MACBETH

30   Don't you know that he has?

MACBETH

We will go no further in this business.
Duncan has honored me lately and I have won
the good opinions of all sorts of people,
which should be worn now like bright new clothes
and not be thrown aside so soon.

LADY MACBETH

35   Was it with drunken hope only
that you dressed yourself? Has your hope fallen asleep?
And does it wake up now, to look so sickly green and pale
at what it decided so easily? From now on
I will consider your love to be equally fickle and undependable.
    Are you afraid
40   to show by action and courage
the man you want to be in your desire? Do you wish to possess
    the thing
that you value most highly in life (i.e., the crown)
and yet live like a coward in your own judgment,
letting "I dare not" hold back "I would,"
like the poor cat in the proverb?

MACBETH

45   I beg you, be quiet!
I dare do all that is fitting for a man to do;
anyone who dares do more is not a man.

LADY MACBETH

What beast was it then
that made you reveal this business to me?
When you dared to do the deed, then you were a man,
50   and if you could be greater than what you were then, you would

Be so much more the man. Nor time nor place
Did then adhere, and yet you would make both.
They have made themselves, and that their fitness now
Does unmake you. I have given suck, and know
55   How tender 'tis to love the babe that milks me.
I would, while it was smiling in my face,
Have plucked my nipple from his boneless gums,
And dashed the brains out, had I so sworn as you
Have done to this.

MACBETH
                    If we should fail?

LADY MACBETH
                              We fail?
60   But screw your courage to the sticking-place,*
And we'll not fail. When Duncan is asleep—
Whereto the rather shall his day's hard journey
Soundly invite him—his two chamberlains
Will I with wine and wassail so convince,
65   That memory, the warder of the brain,
Shall be a fume, and the receipt of reason
A limbeck* only: when in swinish sleep
Their drenchèd natures lie as in a death,
What cannot you and I perform upon
70   Th' unguarded Duncan, what not put upon
His spongy officers, who shall bear the guilt
Of our great quell?

MACBETH
                    Bring forth men-children only;
For thy undaunted mettle should compose
Nothing but males. Will it not be received,
75   When we have marked with blood those sleepy two
Of his own chamber, and used their very daggers,
That they have done 't?

LADY MACBETH
                    Who dares receive it other,
As we shall make our griefs and clamor roar
Upon his death?

---

60   *screw your courage to the sticking-place*   This usage may refer either
to the tightening of strings on a viol as it is tuned or to the screwing up of
the cord on a crossbow to the "sticking-place" (i.e., making it as taut as

be so much more of a man. Then, neither the time nor the place
were suitable, and yet you wished to create both.
Now that they have presented themselves, their very suitableness
has made you impotent. I have suckled a baby and know
55 how tender it is to love the infant that nurses at my breast.
I would rather, while it was smiling in my face,
have plucked my nipple from his toothless mouth
and smashed his brains out, had I sworn as you
have to do this deed (and then denied your promise).

MACBETH
What if we should fail?

LADY MACBETH
We fail?
60 Just tighten your courage until it is taut,
and we won't fail. When Duncan is asleep—
which his hard day's journey
will strongly invite him to—I will so overpower his two servants
with wine and drunken toasts
65 that memory, which should guard the brain,
will become merely a wisp of smoke, and the vessel of reason
    (i.e., the brain)
will only be an empty container. Asleep like swine,
their alcohol-drowned senses numb as if in death—
what can't we two do then to
70 the unguarded Duncan? What blame can't we attach to
his drunken servants, who will be held guilty
of our great murder?

MACBETH
You should be the mother of sons only,
because your fearless spirit should produce
nothing but males. Won't everyone believe—
75 when we have smeared with blood his own
two sleepy servants, and used their very daggers—
that they have done it?

LADY MACBETH
Who will dare take it otherwise,
since we will grieve so noisily and raise such an outcry
at his death?

---

possible and ready to be shot).
  67 *limbeck* alembic, a word derived from the Moorish alchemists of
Spain. It was an instrument used in distillation.

MACBETH

I am settled, and bend up
80   Each corporal agent to this terrible feat.
Away, and mock the time with fairest show:
False face must hide what the false heart doth know.
Exeunt.

Act II, Scene i: [*Inverness. Court of* MACBETH's *castle.*] *Enter*
BANQUO, *and* FLEANCE, *with a torch before him.*

BANQUO
How goes the night, boy?

FLEANCE
The moon is down; I have not heard the clock.

BANQUO
And she goes down at twelve.

FLEANCE

I take't, 'tis later, sir.

BANQUO
5   Hold, take my sword. There's husbandry in heaven.
Their candles are all out. Take thee that too.
A heavy summons lies like lead upon me,
And yet I would not sleep. Merciful powers,
Restrain in me the cursèd thoughts that nature
Gives way to in repose!
Enter MACBETH, *and a Servant with a torch.*
Give me my sword!
10   Who's there?

MACBETH
A friend.

BANQUO
What, sir, not yet at rest? The King's a-bed.
He hath been in unusual pleasure, and
Sent forth great largess to your office.
15   This diamond he greets your wife withal,
By the name of most kind hostess; and shut up
In measureless content.

MACBETH

I am resolved and will exert

80 all my physical energy to this terrible task.

Let's go, and let's fool the world by looking our best;

a deceptive appearance must hide what the deceiving heart
knows.

They exit.

Act II, Scene i: A courtyard in Macbeth's castle. It is night. Enter
BANQUO *and his son,* FLEANCE, *carrying a torch.*

BANQUO

How late is it, boy?

FLEANCE

The moon has gone down. I haven't heard the clock strike.

BANQUO

And the moon goes down at midnight.

FLEANCE

I think it is later than that, sir.

BANQUO

Wait, take my sword. Heaven is thrifty;

5 she's blown out all her candles. (*Hands Fleance something,
    perhaps a dagger.*) Take that too.

The desire to sleep lies as heavy as lead on me,

and yet I don't want to sleep. Merciful angels,

keep away the dreadful thoughts that nature

permits us in our dreams.

Enter MACBETH, *and a Servant with a torch.*

Give me my sword!

10 Who's there?

MACBETH

A friend.

BANQUO

What, sir, haven't you gone to bed yet? The King is already in
his bed.

He has been in an unusually good mood, and

sent generous gifts to your servants.

15 He gives this diamond to your wife with his greeting,

and calls her a most gracious hostess. He has retired

in excellent spirits.

MACBETH

       Being unprepared,
Our will became the servant to defect,
Which else should free have wrought.

BANQUO

          All's well.
20 I dreamt last night of the three Weird Sisters:
To you they have showed some truth.

MACBETH

         I think not of them.
Yet, when we can entreat an hour to serve,
We would spend it in some words upon that business,
If you would grant the time.

BANQUO

      At your kind'st leisure.

MACBETH

25 If you shall cleave to my consent, when 'tis,
It shall make honor for you.

BANQUO

       So I lose none
In seeking to augment it, but still keep
My bosom franchised and allegiance clear,
I shall be counseled.

MACBETH

      Good repose the while!

BANQUO

30 Thanks, sir. The like to you!
   Exit BANQUO [*with* FLEANCE].

MACBETH

Go bid thy mistress, when my drink is ready,
She strike upon the bell. Get thee to bed.
   Exit [*Servant*].
Is this a dagger which I see before me,
The handle toward my hand? Come, let me clutch thee!
35 I have thee not, and yet I see thee still.
Art thou not, fatal vision, sensible
To feeling as to sight, or art thou but

MACBETH
Since we were unprepared,
our wish to serve the King was hampered by our shortcomings;
otherwise, we should have done much more.

BANQUO
Everything is fine.
20   Last night I dreamt of the three Weird Sisters;
they have shown you some measure of truth.

MACBETH
I don't think about them.
Yet, when we can spare an hour for the purpose,
we should discuss this matter,
if you would give me the time.

BANQUO
Whenever it suits you.

MACBETH
25   If you will follow my advice, when the time comes,
it will bring honor to you.

BANQUO
Provided that I lose no honor
in seeking more honors. But if I can continue to keep
my heart innocent and my loyalty spotless,
I would be willing to follow your advice.

MACBETH
Meanwhile, have a good night's sleep.

BANQUO
30   Thanks, sir. The same to you.
        Exit BANQUO *and* FLEANCE.

MACBETH *(to a Servant)*
Go tell Lady Macbeth that when my nightcap is ready,
she should ring the bell. Get to bed.
        Servant exits.
Is this a dagger that I see before me
with its handle turned to my hand? Come, let me grasp you—
35   I can't get hold of you, and yet I still see you.
Deadly vision, can't you
be felt as well as seen, or are you only

A dagger of the mind, a false creation,
Proceeding from the heat-oppressèd brain?
40 I see thee yet, in form as palpable
As this which now I draw.
Thou marshal'st me the way that I was going;
And such an instrument I was to use.
Mine eyes are made the fools o' th' other senses,
45 Or else worth all the rest. I see thee still;
And on thy blade and dudgeon gouts of blood,
Which was not so before. There's no such thing.
It is the bloody business which informs
Thus to mine eyes. Now o'er the one half-world
50 Nature seems dead, and wicked dreams abuse
The curtained sleep. Witchcraft celebrates
Pale Hecate's* offerings; and withered murder,
Alarumed by his sentinel, the wolf,
Whose howl's his watch, thus with his stealthy pace,
55 With Tarquin's* ravishing strides, towards his design
Moves like a ghost. Thou sure and firm-set earth,
Hear not my steps, which way they walk, for fear
Thy very stones prate of my whereabout,
And take the present horror from the time,
60 Which now suits with it. Whiles I threat, he lives:
Words to the heat of deeds too cold breath gives.
        A bell rings.
I go, and it is done. The bell invites me.
Hear it not, Duncan, for it is a knell
That summons thee to heaven, or to hell.
        Exit.

Scene ii: [MACBETH's *Castle.*] *Enter* LADY [MACBETH].

LADY MACBETH
    That which hath made them drunk hath made me bold;
    What hath quenched them hath given me fire. Hark! Peace!
    It was the owl that shrieked, the fatal bellman,

---

52 *Hecate* the classical goddess of magic and witchcraft.
55 *Tarquin* Sextus Tarquinius, noted for his tyranny and arrogance.
When the Roman people (6th century B.C.) saw the virtuous Lucrece stab

a dagger of the mind, a false illusion
created by my feverish brain?

40 I still see you! Your shape is as real
as my own dagger, which I now draw from its sheath.
You lead me in the direction I was going (i.e., to Duncan's
    room),
and it was just such a dagger I was planning to use.
Either my eyes are being made fools of by my other senses,

45 or they are worth all the rest of my senses together. I still
    see you;
and on your blade and hilt, I see large drops of blood
which were not there before. There's no such thing as this
    dagger.
It is this bloody business I am about to do which makes me
see things. Now in one hemisphere of the world,

50 nature seems dead, and wicked dreams disturb
the sleepers in their curtained beds. Witches are performing
    their rites
to pale Hecate; and gaunt murder—
called to action by his watchman, the wolf,
whose howl tells him when to strike—with careful, secret steps,

55 like Tarquin going to rape Lucrece, moves toward his goal
like a ghost. O firm and steady earth,
don't hear my steps, don't see which way they go, for fear that
the stones themselves will tell where I am,
and take away the horror of this moment,

60 which is so right for it. While I make threats, Duncan lives;
words cool the heat of deeds with their cold breath.
    A bell rings.
I go and the murder will be done. The bell urges me to do it.
Don't listen to it, Duncan, for it is a death bell
that calls you to heaven or to hell.
    He exits.

Act II, Scene ii: Macbeth's Castle. Enter LADY MACBETH.

LADY MACBETH
    The wine that has made Duncan's guards drunk has made me
        bold;
    what has drowned them has given me fire. What's that? Listen!
    It was an owl hooting, that fatal night-watchman,

herself after being ravished by Tarquin, they rose and expelled the Tarquin
family from Rome. Shakespeare uses the story in his poem, *The Rape of
Lucrece.*

Which gives the stern'st good-night.* He is about it.
5   The doors are open, and the surfeited grooms
Do mock their charge with snores. I have drugged their possets,
That death and nature do contend about them,
Whether they live or die.

MACBETH [*Within*]

Who's there? What, ho?

LADY MACBETH

Alack, I am afraid they have awaked
10   And 'tis not done! Th' attempt and not the deed
Confounds us. Hark! I laid their daggers ready;
He could not miss 'em. Had he not resembled
My father as he slept, I had done 't.
        Enter MACBETH.

My husband!

MACBETH

I have done the deed. Didst thou not hear a noise?

LADY MACBETH

15   I heard the owl scream and the crickets cry.
Did not you speak?

MACBETH

When?

LADY MACBETH

Now.

MACBETH

As I descended?

LADY MACBETH

Ay.

MACBETH

Hark!
Who lies i' th' second chamber?

LADY MACBETH

Donalbain.

MACBETH

20   This is a sorry sight.

LADY MACBETH

A foolish thought, to say a sorry sight.

---

4   *stern'st good-night*   according to superstition, the owl's hoot foretells
death. In this image the owl is seen as a bellman or towncrier visiting the
condemned prisoner on the night before his execution.

who gives the grimmest good-night. Macbeth is doing the
murder.

5   The doors are open and the drunken guards
seem to mock the King with their snores. I have so drugged
their nightcaps
that life and death are struggling over them, trying to decide
whether they are alive or dead.

MACBETH (*offstage*)
Who's there? What's that?

LADY MACBETH
Alas, I'm afraid the guards have awakened
10   and the murder is not yet done! The attempt and not the deed
itself
will ruin us. But wait! I placed the guards' daggers where
Macbeth could not miss them. If Duncan hadn't looked so much
like
my father as he slept, I would have murdered him myself.
Enter MACBETH.
My husband!

MACBETH
I have done the deed. Didn't you hear a noise?

LADY MACBETH
15   I heard the owl hoot and the crickets chirp.
Didn't you speak?

MACBETH
When?

LADY MACBETH
Now.

MACBETH
As I came down the stairs?

LADY MACBETH
Yes.

MACBETH
Wait!
Who sleeps in the second bedroom?

LADY MACBETH
Donalbain.

MACBETH (*looking at his bloody hands*)
20   This is a miserable sight.

LADY MACBETH
It's foolish to say "a miserable sight."

MACBETH
There's one did laugh in 's sleep, and one cried "Murder!"
That they did wake each other. I stood and heard them.
But they did say their prayers, and addressed them
Again to sleep.

LADY MACBETH
                                    There are two lodged together.

MACBETH
One cried "God bless us!" and "Amen" the other,
As they had seen me with these hangman's hands:
List'ning their fear, I could not say "Amen,"
When they did say "God bless us!"

LADY MACBETH
                                    Consider it not so deeply.

MACBETH
But wherefore could not I pronounce "Amen"?
I had most need of blessing, and "Amen"
Stuck in my throat.

LADY MACBETH
                              These deeds must not be thought
After these ways; so, it will make us mad.

MACBETH
Methought I heard a voice cry "Sleep no more!
Macbeth does murder sleep"—the innocent sleep,
Sleep that knits up the raveled sleave of care,
The death of each day's life, sore labor's bath,
Balm of hurt minds, great nature's second course,
Chief nourisher in life's feast——

LADY MACBETH
                                    What do you mean?

MACBETH
Still it cried "Sleep no more!" to all the house:
"Glamis hath murdered sleep, and therefore Cawdor
Shall sleep no more: Macbeth shall sleep no more!"

LADY MACBETH
Who was it that thus cried? Why, worthy thane,
You do unbend your noble strength, to think

MACBETH
> One of the guards laughed in his sleep and another cried
>> "Murder!"—
> the two of them woke each other up. Standing there, I heard
>> them.
> Then they said their prayers and went
> to sleep again.

LADY MACBETH

> There are two of them sleeping in that room.

MACBETH
> One cried "God bless us!" and the other replied "Amen."
> It was as if they had seen me with these bloody hands of a
>> hangman.
> Listening to their fearful prayers, I couldn't say "Amen"
> to their "God bless us!"

LADY MACBETH
> Don't think about it so seriously.

MACBETH
> But why couldn't I say "Amen"?
> I had the strongest need to be blessed, yet "Amen"
> stuck in my throat.

LADY MACBETH
> We must not think about these deeds
> in this way or it will drive us mad.

MACBETH
> I thought I heard a voice cry "Sleep no more!
> Macbeth has murdered sleep"—the innocent sleep,
> sleep that straightens and rewinds the tangled yarn of care,
> the death of each day's life, a fresh bath after hard work,
> a healing salve for disturbed minds, the main course at great
>> nature's dinner,
> the chief nourishment in life's feast—

LADY MACBETH
> What do you mean?

MACBETH
> The voice still cried "Sleep no more!" shouting it all over the
>> house.
> "Glamis has murdered sleep, and therefore Cawdor
> shall sleep no more; Macbeth shall sleep no more."

LADY MACBETH
> Who was it that cried out this way? Worthy thane, why
> do you sap your noble strength by thinking

25

30

35

40

45   So brainsickly of things. Go get some water,
      And wash this filthy witness from your hand.
      Why did you bring these daggers from the place?
      They must lie there. Go carry them, and smear
      The sleepy grooms with blood.

MACBETH
                          I'll go no more.
50   I am afraid to think what I have done;
      Look on 't again I dare not.

LADY MACBETH
                          Infirm of purpose!
      Give me the daggers. The sleeping and the dead
      Are but as pictures. 'Tis the eye of childhood
      That fears a painted devil. If he do bleed,
55   I'll gild the faces of the grooms withal,
      For it must seem their guilt.
              Exit. Knock within.

MACBETH
                          Whence is that knocking?
      How is 't with me, when every noise appalls me?
      What hands are here? Ha! They pluck out mine eyes!
      Will all great Neptune's* ocean wash this blood
60   Clean from my hand? No; this my hand will rather
      The multitudinous seas incarnadine,
      Making the green one, red.
              Enter LADY [MACBETH].

LADY MACBETH
      My hands are of your color, but I shame
      To wear a heart so white. (*Knock.*) I hear a knocking
65   At the south entry. Retire we to our chamber.
      A little water clears us of this deed:
      How easy is it then! Your constancy
      Hath left you unattended. (*Knock.*) Hark! more knocking.
      Get on your nightgown, lest occasion call us
70   And show us to be watchers. Be not lost
      So poorly in your thoughts.

---

59 *Neptune* the Roman god of the sea.

45 so insanely about what you have done? Go, get some water
and wash this bloody evidence from your hands.
Why did you bring these daggers from Duncan's room?
They must remain there. Go take them back and smear
the sleeping guards with Duncan's blood.

MACBETH
I won't go back there again.
50 I am afraid even to think what I have done; I don't dare to look
at it again.

LADY MACBETH
Weak-willed creature!
Give me the daggers. Persons sleeping or dead
are only like paintings. It is childish
to fear a painted devil. If Duncan bleeds,
I'll paint the guards' faces with the blood,
55 because they must appear to be guilty of his murder.
        Exit LADY MACBETH. *Knocking is heard offstage.*

MACBETH
Where is that knocking coming from?
What is the matter with me that every noise terrifies me?
(*Looking at his hands*) Whose hands are these? Ha! They tear
out my eyes!
Can all great Neptune's ocean wash this blood
from off my hand? No. This hand, instead, will
60 dye the huge and mighty seas crimson,
turning the green ocean red.
        Enter LADY MACBETH.

LADY MACBETH
My hands are the same color as yours, but I would be ashamed
to have a heart so white with cowardice. (*Knocking offstage.*)
I hear knocking
at the south gate. Let us go to our bedroom.
65 A little water will clear us of this murder (by washing away the
bloody evidence).
It will all be so easy then! Your usual firm will
has deserted you. (*Knocking.*) Listen! More knocking.
Put on your robe in case we are called for
and it is discovered that we have been up. Don't be so
70 weak-mindedly lost in your thoughts.

MACBETH

    To know my deed, 'twere best not know myself. (*Knock.*)
    Wake Duncan with thy knocking! I would thou couldst!
    Exeunt.

Scene iii: [MACBETH'S *Castle.*] *Enter a Porter. Knocking within.*

PORTER

    Here's a knocking indeed! If a man were porter of hell gate,
    he should have old turning the key. (*Knock.*) Knock, knock,
    knock! Who's there, i' th' name of Beelzebub?* Here's a farmer,
    that hanged himself on th' expectation of plenty.* Come in time!
5   Have napkins enow about you; here you'll sweat for 't. (*Knock.*)
    Knock, knock! Who's there, in th' other devil's name. Faith,
    here's an equivocator,* that could swear in both the scales against
    either scale; who committed treason enough for God's sake, yet
    could not equivocate to heaven. O, come in, equivocator.
10 (*Knock.*) Knock, knock, knock! Who's there? Faith, here's an
    English tailor come hither for stealing out of a French hose:*
    come in, tailor. Here you may roast your goose.* (*Knock.*)
    Knock, knock; never at quiet! What are you? But this place is
    too cold for hell. I'll devil-porter it no further. I had thought to
15 have let in some of all professions that go the primrose way to
    th' everlasting bonfire. (*Knock.*) Anon, anon! [*Open an en-
    trance.*] I pray you, remember the porter.
        Enter MACDUFF *and* LENNOX.

---

    3 *Beelzebub* in Matthew xii:24, Beelzebub is spoken of as "the prince
of the devils." Milton gives the name to one of the fallen angels next to
Satan in power (*Paradise Lost*, I, 79).
    4 *expectation of plenty* probably means that the farmer expected to
sell hoarded grain at high prices, but abundant crops caused the supply to
exceed the demand and he lost his investment.
    7 *equivocator* one who uses double-meanings to confuse his listeners.
Shakespeare may have had in mind the Jesuit, Henry Garnet, Superior of
the Society of Jesus in England. He stood trial on March 28, 1606, for
participating in the Gunpowder Plot (a plan to blow up Parliament in
retaliation for anti-Catholic laws). He later confessed to equivocating at
the trial—to perjury his enemies said—and was hanged.
    11 *French hose* certain types of French trousers fitted so tightly that
even a dishonest tailor had trouble stealing surplus material while making
them.
    12 *goose* tailor's pressing iron.

MACBETH

To acknowledge what I've done, I would have to suppress all
knowledge of myself.
Knocking.
Wake Duncan with your knocking! I wish you could!
They exit.

*Act II, Scene iii: Macbeth's Castle. The knocking from offstage
continues. Enter a drunken Gate-keeper.*

GATE-KEEPER

What a knocking this is! If a man were gate-keeper of the
entrance to hell,
he'd certainly have plenty of key-turning. (*Knocking.*) Knock,
knock,
knock! Who's there in the name of Beelzebub? (*Imagining
himself as the Gate-keeper of hell.*) Here comes a farmer
who hanged himself for speculating unwisely on a good harvest
of wheat. You come at a good time!
5 Bring enough towels; you'll sweat down here for committing
suicide. (*Knocking.*)
Knock, knock! Who's there in the name of the other devil?
It's a double-dealing Jesuit who can use the pro and con of an
argument for
whichever side he prefers. He's betrayed his country for God's
sake, yet
he can't double-talk his way into heaven. Welcome, equivocator.
10 (*Knocking.*) Knock, knock, knock! Who's there? By Jove, it's an
English tailor sent here for cheating by skimping on the amount
of cloth used in making French pants.
Do come in tailor; here, you have heat enough to roast your
goose. (*Knocking.*)
Knock, knock! Never a moment's peace. Who are you?—But this
place is
too cold for hell. I won't play the devil's Gate-keeper any longer.
I had hoped to
15 let in some from all the professions that are going down the
primrose path to
the everlasting fire of hell. (*Knocking.*) Coming, coming. (*Opens
the gate.*) I beg you, remember a tip for the Gate-keeper.
Enter MACDUFF *and* LENNOX.

MACDUFF
Was it so late, friend, ere you went to bed,
That you do lie so late?

PORTER
20   Faith, sir, we were carousing till the second cock:* and drink,
sir, is a great provoker of three things.

MACDUFF
What three things does drink especially provoke?

PORTER
Marry, sir, nose-painting, sleep, and urine. Lechery, sir, it provokes and unprovokes; it provokes the desire, but it takes away
25   the performance: therefore much drink may be said to be an
equivocator with lechery: it makes him and it mars him; it sets
him on and it takes him off; it persuades him and disheartens
him; makes him stand to and not stand to; in conclusion,
equivocates him in a sleep, and giving him the lie, leaves him.

MACDUFF
30   I believe drink gave thee the lie last night.

PORTER
That it did, sir, i' the very throat on me: but I requited him for
his lie, and, I think, being too strong for him, though he took
up my legs sometime, yet I made a shift to cast him.

MACDUFF
Is thy master stirring?
    Enter MACBETH.
35   Our knocking has awaked him; here he comes.

LENNOX
Good morrow, noble sir.

MACBETH
                    Good morrow, both.

MACDUFF
Is the king stirring, worthy thane?

MACBETH
                    Not yet.

---

20   *second cock*   second cockcrow or about 3 A.M.

MACDUFF

You must have gone to bed pretty late, friend,

that you sleep so late?

GATE-KEEPER

20   Believe me, sir, we were celebrating until the wee early hours;
     and drink,

sir, is a great stimulator of three things.

MACDUFF

What three things does drink especially stimulate?

GATE-KEEPER

Indeed sir, red noses, sleep, and urine. Sex, sir, it

stimulates and unstimulates: it stimulates the desire, but it
takes away

25   the ability to perform. Therefore, much drink may be said to be a
     double-dealer with sex: it helps him and it hinders him; it gets

him going and it stops him in his tracks; it encourages him and
discourages

him; makes him stand firm and not stand firm. In conclusion,
drink double-deals the drinker into sleep and having deceived
him, leaves him.

MACDUFF

30   I believe drink tricked you last night.

GATE-KEEPER

That it did sir, in the most profound sort of way, but I repaid
him for

it, I think, by being too strong for him. Though at one point
he had

me by the legs, I pulled my trick and vomited him out.

MACDUFF

Is your master up?

          Enter MACBETH.

35   Our knocking has awakened him; here he comes.

LENNOX

Good morning, noble sir.

MACBETH

Good morning to you both.

MACDUFF

Is the King up yet, worthy thane?

MACBETH

Not yet.

MACDUFF
He did command me to call timely on him:
I have almost slipped the hour.

MACBETH
                                    I'll bring you to him.

MACDUFF
40   I know this is a joyful trouble to you;
But yet 'tis one.

MACBETH
The labor we delight in physics pain.
This is the door.

MACDUFF
                        I'll make so bold to call,
For 'tis my limited service.
        Exit MACDUFF.

LENNOX
Goes the king hence today?

MACBETH
45   He does: he did appoint so.

LENNOX
The night has been unruly. Where we lay,
Our chimneys were blown down, and, as they say,
Lamentings heard i' th' air, strange screams of death,
And prophesying with accents terrible
50   Of dire combustion and confused events
New hatched to th' woeful time. The obscure bird
Clamored the livelong night. Some say, the earth
Was feverous and did shake.

MACBETH
                                'Twas a rough night.

LENNOX
My young remembrance cannot parallel
55   A fellow to it.
        Enter MACDUFF.

MACDUFF
O horror, horror, horror! Tongue nor heart
Cannot conceive nor name thee.

MACBETH *AND* LENNOX
                                What's the matter?

MACDUFF

He ordered me to call on him early in the morning.
I almost let the time slip by.

MACBETH

I'll bring you to him.

MACDUFF

40   I know your hospitality has been a joyful trouble for you,
but yet it still has been trouble.

MACBETH

Things we like to do negate our idea of trouble.
Here's the door (to Duncan's room).

MACDUFF

I'm going to take the liberty of waking him,
since it's my appointed task.
    Exit MACDUFF.

LENNOX

Will the King be leaving today?

MACBETH

45   He will. At least that was his intention.

LENNOX

It's been a fierce night. Where we were sleeping,
our chimneys were blown down, and they say that
weeping was heard in the air, strange death-screams
and prophecies in frightful voices
50   of dreadful tumult and chaos,
which would be born out of these sorrowful times. The owl
hooted all night long. Some say the earth
quaked as if it had a fever.

MACBETH

It was a rough night.

LENNOX

I can't remember anything like it
55   in my short life.
    Enter MACDUFF.

MACDUFF

O horror, horror, horror! The heart cannot understand
nor the tongue name this horror.

MACBETH *and* LENNOX

What's the matter?

MACDUFF

>Confusion now hath made his masterpiece.
>Most sacrilegious murder hath broke ope
>60 The Lord's anointed temple, and stole thence
>The life o' th' building.

MACBETH

>   What is 't you say? The life?

LENNOX

>Mean you his Majesty?

MACDUFF

>Approach the chamber, and destroy your sight
>With a new Gorgon:* do not bid me speak;
>65 See, and then speak yourselves. Awake, awake!

>*Exeunt* MACBETH *and* LENNOX.

>Ring the alarum bell. Murder and treason!
>Banquo and Donalbain! Malcolm! Awake!
>Shake off this downy sleep, death's counterfeit,
>And look on death itself! Up, up, and see
>70 The great doom's image! Malcolm! Banquo!
>As from your graves rise up, and walk like sprites,
>To countenance this horror. Ring the bell!

>*Bell rings. Enter* LADY [MACBETH].

LADY MACBETH

>   What's the business,
>That such a hideous trumpet calls to parley
>The sleepers of the house? Speak, speak!

MACDUFF

>75   O gentle lady,
>'Tis not for you to hear what I can speak:
>The repetition, in a woman's ear,
>Would murder as it fell.

>*Enter* BANQUO.

>   O Banquo, Banquo!
>Our royal master's murdered.

LADY MACBETH

>   Woe, alas!
>What, in our house?

---

64 *Gorgon* according to Greek mythology, the Gorgon was a monster, the sight of which turned the beholder to stone.

MACDUFF

Dire destruction has created its masterpiece.
Sacrilegious murder has ripped open
60 our Lord's anointed flesh and stolen
the life from the body.

MACBETH

What are you saying? The life?

LENNOX

Do you mean his Majesty?

MACDUFF

Go to his bedroom and be blinded
by a new Gorgon. Don't ask me to speak.
65 See for yourselves and speak. Awake! Awake!
        Exit MACBETH *and* LENNOX.
Sound the alarm bell. Murder and treason!
Banquo and Donalbain! Malcolm! Wake up!
Shake off this sleep, soft as down, the image of death,
and look upon death itself. Get up and see
70 the likeness of Judgment Day. Malcolm! Banquo!
Rise up as if leaving your graves
and look upon this horror! Ring the bell!
        Bell rings.
        Enter LADY MACBETH.

LADY MACBETH

What's going on
that such a hideous alarm bell calls
the sleepers of this house to talk together? Speak, speak!

MACDUFF

75 O gentle lady,
it is not for you to hear what I could say.
The reciting of it in a woman's ear
would kill her as she heard it.
        Enter BANQUO.
O Banquo, Banquo,
our royal master's murdered!

LADY MACBETH

O woe is me, alas!
And in our house?

BANQUO
                    Too cruel anywhere.
Dear Duff, I prithee, contradict thyself,
And say it is not so.
        Enter MACBETH, LENNOX, *and* ROSS.
MACBETH
Had I but died an hour before this chance,
I had lived a blessèd time; for from this instant
There's nothing serious in mortality:
All is but toys. Renown and grace is dead,
The wine of life is drawn, and the mere lees
Is left this vault to brag of.
        Enter MALCOLM *and* DONALBAIN.
DONALBAIN
What is amiss?
MACBETH
              You are, and do not know 't.
The spring, the head, the fountain of your blood
Is stopped; the very source of it is stopped.
MACDUFF
Your royal father's murdered.
MALCOLM
                  O, by whom?
LENNOX
Those of his chamber, as it seemed, had done 't:
Their hands and faces were all badged with blood;
So were their daggers, which unwiped we found
Upon their pillows. They stared, and were distracted.
No man's life was to be trusted with them.
MACBETH
O, yet I do repent me of my fury,
That I did kill them.
MACDUFF
             Wherefore did you so?
MACBETH
Who can be wise, amazed, temp'rate and furious,
Loyal and neutral, in a moment? No man.
The expedition of my violent love
Outrun the pauser, reason. Here lay Duncan,

BANQUO

80   Such a murder is too cruel anywhere.
Dear Macduff, I beg you to contradict yourself
and say it is not so.

Enter MACBETH, LENNOX, *and* ROSS.

MACBETH

If I had died an hour before this happened,
I would have lived a happy life. From this moment on
there is no serious meaning to life.

85   Everything is a mere trifle. Fame and honor are dead.
The wine of life has been spilled and only the dregs
are left for this wine-cellar of a world to boast of.

Enter MALCOLM *and* DONALBAIN.

DONALBAIN

What's wrong?

MACBETH

You are, and you do not know it.
The source, the origin, the fountain of your blood,

90   is stopped up; its very spring is destroyed.

MACDUFF

Your royal father has been murdered.

MALCOLM

O, by whom?

LENNOX

It appears that his bedroom guards did it.
Their hands and faces were all smeared with blood,
and so were their daggers, which were found unwiped

95   upon their pillows. They stared and looked confused.
No man's life was safe with them.

MACBETH

And yet I am sorry that in my fury
I killed them.

MACDUFF

Why did you do it?

MACBETH

Who can be wise, bewildered, cool-headed and furious,

100   loyal and indifferent, all at the same time? No man can.
The impulsiveness of my violent love
outran my reason, which normally makes me hesitate. Duncan
    lay here,

His silver skin laced with his golden blood,
105   And his gashed stabs looked like a breach in nature
For ruin's wasteful entrance: there, the murderers,
Steeped in the colors of their trade, their daggers
Unmannerly breeched with gore. Who could refrain,
That had a heart to love, and in that heart
Courage to make 's love known?

LADY MACBETH

110   Help me hence, ho!

MACDUFF

Look to the lady.

MALCOLM [*Aside to Donalbain*]
                     Why do we hold our tongues,
That most may claim this argument for ours?

DONALBAIN [*Aside to Malcolm*]
    What should be spoken here,
Where our fate, hid in an auger-hole,
115   May rush, and seize us? Let's away.
Our tears are not yet brewed.

MALCOLM [*Aside to Donalbain*]
                     Nor our strong sorrow
Upon the foot of motion.

BANQUO
                 Look to the lady.

[LADY MACBETH *is carried out.*]
And when we have our naked frailties hid,
That suffer in exposure, let us meet
120   And question this most bloody piece of work,
To know it further. Fears and scruples shake us.
In the great hand of God I stand, and thence
Against the undivulged pretense I fight
Of treasonous malice.

MACDUFF
               And so do I.

ALL
                  So all.

MACBETH
125   Let's briefly put on manly readiness,
And meet i' th' hall together.

his silver skin streaked with his golden blood,
105   and his gashed wounds looked like a gap in the natural creation
through which destruction could enter. The murderers lay there,
soaked in the bloody colors of their trade, their daggers
obscenely clothed in blood like breeches. Who could control
    himself
that had a loving heart and in that heart
the courage to show it?

LADY MACBETH (*fainting*)
110   Help me out of here.

MACDUFF
Look after the lady.

MALCOLM (*to his brother Donalbain*)
Why do we keep quiet
who are most concerned with this subject?

DONALBAIN (*to Malcolm*)
What can we dare to say in this place,
where our own destiny, hidden in a tiny hole,
115   may rush out and seize us? Let's go away.
This is not the right time for us to express our grief (which will
    reach its climax later).

MALCOLM (*to Donalbain*)
And neither has our great sorrow
yet begun to show itself.

BANQUO
Look after the lady.
        LADY MACBETH *is carried out.*
When we have properly clothed our frail bodies,
that shake in the cold air, let us meet
120   and discuss this most bloody piece of work
to understand it further. Fears and doubts are shaking all of us.
I place myself in God's great hand, and with His support
I vow to fight against the undiscovered motives
of treason and evil intent.

MACDUFF
And so do I.

ALL
So do all of us.

MACBETH
125   Let's quickly put on our armor
and meet together in the great hall of the castle.

ALL

                                Well contented

             Exeunt [all but MALCOLM *and* DONALBAIN].

MALCOLM

        What will you do? Let's not consort with them.
        To show an unfelt sorrow is an office
        Which the false man does easy. I'll to England.

DONALBAIN

130   To Ireland, I; our separated fortune
        Shall keep us both the safer. Where we are
        There's daggers in men's smiles; the near in blood,
        The nearer bloody.

MALCOLM

                          This murderous shaft that's shot
        Hath not yet lighted, and our safest way
135   Is to avoid the aim. Therefore to horse!
        And let us not be dainty of leave-taking,
        But shift away. There's warrant in that theft
        Which steals itself when there's no mercy left.

                Exeunt.

Scene iv: [Outside MACBETH'S *castle.] Enter* ROSS *with an Old
Man.*

OLD MAN

        Threescore and ten I can remember well:
        Within the volume of which time I have seen
        Hours of dreadful and things strange, but this sore night
        Hath trifled former knowings.

ROSS

                                Ha, good father,
5   Thou seest the heavens, as troubled with man's act,
        Threatens his bloody stage. By th' clock 'tis day,
        And yet dark night strangles the traveling lamp:
        Is 't night's predominance, or the day's shame,
        That darkness does the face of earth entomb,
        When living light should kiss it?

ALL

Agreed!

All exit except MALCOLM *and* DONALBAIN.

MALCOLM

What will you do? Let's not get together with them.
To show sorrow you don't feel is an act
which comes easily to a hypocrite. I'm going to England.

DONALBAIN

130 And I'm going to Ireland. By going our separate ways,
we shall both be safer. Wherever the two of us are,
men's smiles conceal daggers. The closer the relative,
the nearer he is to spilling our blood.

MALCOLM

The murdering arrow that has been shot
has not yet reached its goal and it is safest for us
135 to avoid being the target. Therefore, let's get on our horses;
and let us not be too well-mannered in saying farewell
but simply steal away. The thief has the right to steal,
who steals himself away from a place where there is no mercy
left.

They exit.

Act II, Scene iv: Outside Macbeth's Castle. Enter ROSS, *talking
to an old man on the morning after the murder of* DUNCAN.

OLD MAN

My memory goes back seventy years,
in which time I've seen
some dreadful things and peculiar goings-on, but this painful
night
has made everything that has gone before seem like nothing.

ROSS

Well, old fellow,
5 you see the heavens, troubled by man's sins,
punishing this bloody world. According to the clock it's day,
and yet the darkness of night snuffs out that traveling lamp,
the sun.
Is it because night is stronger than day, or is it because of the
day's shame
that darkness buries the face of the earth
when living light should be kissing it?

OLD MAN

'Tis unnatural,
Even like the deed that's done. On Tuesday last
A falcon,* tow'ring in her pride of place,
Was by a mousing owl hawked at and killed.

ROSS

And Duncan's horses—a thing most strange and certain—
Beauteous and swift, the minions of their race,
Turned wild in nature, broke their stalls, flung out,
Contending 'gainst obedience, as they would make
War with mankind.

OLD MAN

'Tis said they ate each other.

ROSS

They did so, to th' amazement of mine eyes,
That looked upon 't.

Enter Macduff.

Here comes the good Macduff.
How goes the world, sir, now?

MACDUFF

Why, see you not?

ROSS

Is 't known who did this more than bloody deed?

MACDUFF

Those that Macbeth hath slain.

ROSS

Alas, the day!
What good could they pretend?

MACDUFF

They were suborned:
Malcolm and Donalbain, the king's two sons,
Are stol'n away and fled, which puts upon them
Suspicion of the deed.

ROSS

'Gainst nature still.
Thriftless ambition, that will ravin up
Thine own life's means! Then 'tis most like
The sovereignty will fall upon Macbeth.

---

12 *falcon* any of various hawks, used for hunting in the sport of hawking or falconry. These birds were trained to pursue and attack wild fowl or game.

OLD MAN
It's as unnatural
as the murder that's just been done. Last Tuesday
a falcon, flying at her highest point,
was swooped on and killed by a mouse-hunting owl.

ROSS
And Duncan's horses—strange to tell but definitely true—
beautiful and swift, the finest of their breed,
became wild, broke out of their stalls, and leaped about,
struggling against all discipline, as if they wanted
to make war against human beings.

OLD MAN
Some say they ate each other.

ROSS
That's what they did, to my utter astonishment—
I saw it with my own eyes.
        Enter MACDUFF.
Here comes good Macduff.
How are things going now, sir?

MACDUFF
Can't you use your own eyes?

ROSS
Is it known yet who committed this more than bloody murder?

MACDUFF
It was the two whom Macbeth has killed.

ROSS
What a sad day it is!
What possible advantage could they get out of it?

MACDUFF
They were bribed.
Malcolm and Donalbain, the king's two sons,
have stolen away and fled, and this puts them under
suspicion of having done it themselves.

ROSS
Another unnatural act!
Reckless ambition that gobbles up
its own flesh! Then it is most likely that
Macbeth will be chosen king.

MACDUFF
  He is already named, and gone to Scone*
  To be invested.
ROSS
                    Where is Duncan's body?
MACDUFF
  Carried to Colmekill,*
  The sacred storehouse of his predecessors
  And guardian of their bones.
ROSS
                              Will you to Scone?
35
MACDUFF
  No, cousin, I'll to Fife.*
ROSS
                    Well, I will thither.
MACDUFF
  Well, may you see things well done there. Adieu,
  Lest our old robes sit easier than our new!
ROSS
  Farewell, father.
OLD MAN
40
  God's benison go with you, and with those
  That would make good of bad, and friends of foes!
                    Exeunt omnes.

Act III, Scene i: [Forres. The palace.] Enter BANQUO.

BANQUO
  Thou hast it now—King, Cawdor, Glamis, all,
  As the weird women promised, and I fear
  Thou play'dst most foully for 't. Yet it was said
  It should not stand in thy posterity,
5
  But that myself should be the root and father
  Of many kings. If there come truth from them—
  As upon thee, Macbeth, their speeches shine—
  Why, by the verities on thee made good,
  May they not be my oracles as well
10
  And set me up in hope? But hush, no more!
                    Sennet sounded. Enter MACBETH *as King,* LADY [MACBETH],
                    LENNOX, ROSS, *Lords, and Attendants.*

_____

  31   *Scone*   ancient capital, near Perth, where the kings of Scotland were
crowned.
  33   *Colmekill*   island cell of St. Columba, now known as Iona, where

MACDUFF

He has already been elected and gone to Scone
to be crowned.

ROSS

Where is Duncan's body?

MACDUFF

It has been carried to Colmekill,
the sacred shrine of his ancestors
and the resting place of their bones.

ROSS

35   Are you going to Scone?

MACDUFF

No, kinsman, I'm off to Fife.

ROSS

Well, I'm going to Scone.

MACDUFF

I hope you see things properly done there. Goodbye.
I fear that Duncan's rule was much better than what we can
    expect from Macbeth's new regime.

ROSS

Goodbye, old fellow.

OLD MAN

40   God's blessing be with you and with those
that make the best of a bad thing, and make friends of foes.
      They exit.

Act III, Scene i: The royal palace at Forres. Enter BANQUO.

BANQUO

You've got it now—King of Scotland, Cawdor, Glamis, all—
just as the fateful witches promised, and I'm afraid
that you played a crooked hand to get it. Yet they also said
that the kingship would not continue to your children,
5   but that I would be the founder and father of
a royal line. If the witches speak true—
and what they said has certainly come true for you, Macbeth—
why, by the truths which have been fulfilled,
why can't the witches be reading my future correctly, too,
10   and therefore raise my own hopes? But hush, no more about this!
      A trumpet fanfare is played. Enter MACBETH *as King,*
      LADY MACBETH *as Queen,* LENNOX, ROSS, *Lords,*
      and Attendants.

Scottish kings were buried.
36 *Fife* in eastern Scotland. Macduff chooses to go to his own castle
rather than to Scone and the coronation.

MACBETH
　Here's our chief guest.
LADY MACBETH
　　　　　　　　　If he had been forgotten,
　It had been as a gap in our great feast,
　And all-thing unbecoming.
MACBETH
　Tonight we hold a solemn supper, sir,
　And I'll request your presence.
BANQUO
　　　　　　　　　　Let your Highness
15　Command upon me, to the which my duties
　Are with a most indissoluble tie
　For ever knit.
MACBETH
　Ride you this afternoon?
BANQUO
　　　　　　　　Ay, my good lord.
MACBETH
20　We should have else desired your good advice
　Which still hath been both grave and prosperous
　In this day's council; but we'll take tomorrow.
　Is 't far you ride?
BANQUO
　As far, my lord, as will fill up the time
25　'Twixt this and supper. Go not my horse the better,
　I must become a borrower of the night
　For a dark hour or twain.
MACBETH
　　　　　　　　　Fail not our feast.
BANQUO
　My lord, I will not.
MACBETH
　We hear our bloody cousins are bestowed
30　In England and in Ireland, not confessing
　Their cruel parricide, filling their hearers
　With strange invention. But of that tomorrow,
　When therewithal we shall have cause of state
　Craving us jointly. Hie you to horse. Adieu,
35　Till you return at night. Goes Fleance with you?

MACBETH
Here's our guest of honor.
LADY MACBETH
If we had forgotten to invite him,
it would have made a gap in our great feast
and have been altogether unfitting.
MACBETH (*to Banquo*)
Tonight we are having an official banquet, sir,
and I personally request your presence.
BANQUO
15   Your Highness
may command me, knowing that my duties
and your commands are, by an unbreakable bond,
forever joined.
MACBETH
Are you riding somewhere this afternoon?
BANQUO
Yes, my good lord.
MACBETH
20   I could have used your good advice,
which has always been wise and useful,
in today's council meeting. Well, we'll take it tomorrow.
Are you riding far?
BANQUO
Far enough, my lord, to take up the time from now
25   until supper. Unless my horse goes faster than usual,
I'll still be riding an hour or two
after sunset.
MACBETH
Make sure to be at our feast.
BANQUO
I'll be there, my lord.
MACBETH
I hear that our murderous kinsmen, Malcolm and Donalbain,
have taken refuge:
30   one in England, the other in Ireland. Instead of confessing
the cruel assassination of their father, they have been spreading
wild tales. But we'll talk about that tomorrow,
along with other matters of state
demanding both your attention and mine. Hurry to your horse.
Goodbye,
35   until you return tonight. Is your son Fleance going with you?

BANQUO

Ay, my good lord. Our time does call upon 's.

MACBETH

I wish your horses swift and sure of foot,
And so I do commend you to their backs.
Farewell.

Exit BANQUO.

40   Let every man be master of this time
Till seven at night. To make society
The sweeter welcome, we will keep ourself
Till supper-time alone. While then, God be with you!

Exeunt Lords [*and all but* MACBETH *and a Servant*].

Sirrah, a word with you: attend those men

45   Our pleasure?

SERVANT

They are, my lord, without the palace gate.

MACBETH

Bring them before us.

Exit Servant.

To be thus is nothing, but to be safely thus—
Our fears in Banquo stick deep,

50   And in his royalty of nature reigns that
Which would be feared. 'Tis much he dares;
And, to that dauntless temper of his mind,
He hath a wisdom that doth guide his valor
To act in safety. There is none but he

55   Whose being I do fear: and under him
My genius is rebuked, as it is said
Mark Antony's was by Cæsar.* He chid the Sisters,
When first they put the name of King upon me,
And bade them speak to him. Then prophet-like

60   They hailed him father to a line of kings.
Upon my head they placed a fruitless crown
And put a barren scepter* in my gripe,
Thence to be wrenched with an unlineal hand,
No son of mine succeeding. If 't be so,

65   For Banquo's issue have I filed my mind;
For them the gracious Duncan have I murdered;

55-57   *under him ... Caesar* referring to a passage in Plutarch's life of
Antony, which observes that Antony always failed in contests with Octavius
Caesar. Shakespeare paraphrases the passage in *Antony and Cleopatra*,

BANQUO
Yes, my good lord. And it is time we got started.

MACBETH
May your horses be swift and sure-footed,
and I wish you well on your journey.
Farewell.
  Exit BANQUO.
40 Let every man pass the time as he wishes
until seven tonight. To make seeing you again
all the more pleasurable, I'll stay by myself
until supper-time. Until then, good luck to you.
  All leave except MACBETH *and a Servant.*
I wish a word with you, my good fellow. Are those men awaiting
45 my orders?

SERVANT
They are, my lord, outside the palace gate.

MACBETH
Bring them to me.
  Exit Servant.
To be king is nothing, unless one is safely king.
My fears about Banquo are deep-rooted.
50 There is something kingly in his nature
which is threatening to me. He dares many things,
and besides the fearless quality of his spirit,
he has a certain wisdom that guides his courage
into acting cautiously. There is no one but him
55 whom I fear. Next to him,
my ruling spirit is overwhelmed, just as they say
Mark Antony's was by Caesar's. Banquo scolded the Witches
when they first called me King,
and ordered them to speak to him. Like prophets,
60 they greeted him as the founder of a royal line.
They put a sterile crown on my head
and a barren scepter in my fist—
both to be torn from me by a stranger, rather than
passed on to one of my sons. If this is true,
65 then I have debased my mind for Banquo's children;
I have murdered the virtuous Duncan for their sake,

II, iii, 10-38.
 62 *scepter* a staff or baton carried by a sovereign that signifies his
royal authority.

Put rancors in the vessel of my peace
Only for them, and mine eternal jewel
Given to the common enemy of man,
70   To make them kings, the seeds of Banquo kings!
Rather than so, come, fate, into the list,
And champion me to th' utterance!* Who's there?
      Enter Servant and Two Murderers.
Now go to the door, and stay there till we call.
      Exit Servant.
Was it not yesterday we spoke together?
MURDERERS
It was, so please your Highness.
MACBETH
75   Well then, now
'Have you considered of my speeches? Know
That it was he in the times past, which held you
So under fortune, which you thought had been
Our innocent self: this I made good to you
80   In our last conference; passed in probation with you,
How you were borne in hand, how crossed; the instruments,
Who wrought with them, and all things else that might
To half a soul and to a notion crazed
Say "Thus did Banquo."
FIRST MURDERER
                              You made it known to us.
MACBETH
85   I did so; and went further, which is now
Our point of second meeting. Do you find
Your patience so predominant in your nature,
That you can let this go? Are you so gospeled,
To pray for this good man and for his issue,
90   Whose heavy hand hath bowed you to the grave
And beggared yours forever?
FIRST MURDERER
                              We are men, my liege.
MACBETH
Ay, in the catalogue ye go for men;
As hounds and greyhounds, mongrels, spaniels, curs,

---

72 *champion me to th' utterance* fight to the uttermost or extremity.
"Utterance" derives from the French "à l'outrance," a chivalric term meaning
combat to the death.

and poisoned my peaceful soul
only for them. My immortal soul
I have given to the devil,
70   to make them kings—the children of Banquo, kings!
Rather than let that happen, let fate enter the tournament
and meet me face to face in mortal combat. Who's there?
Enter Servant and two Murderers.
(*To the Servant*) Go to the door and stay there till I call.
Exit Servant.
Didn't we speak to each other yesterday?

MURDERERS
Yes we did, your Highness.

MACBETH
75   Well then,
have you thought now about what I told you? You know
that in the past, it was Banquo who hindered
your careers, even though I, whom you thought responsible,
was innocent. This I already proved to you
80   at our last meeting, when we looked over the evidence together
of how you had been tricked, how stymied, what means were
    used,
the persons who engineered your downfall, and everything else
    that might,
even to a half-wit or a mad man,
say "Banquo did it."

FIRST MURDERER
You gave us all that information.

MACBETH
85   Yes I did, and I went further, and that
is the point of this second meeting. Is
patience so dominant in your nature
that you can permit such abuse? Are you such good Christians
that you can pray for this man and his offspring,
90   whose strong force has almost pushed you into the grave
and impoverished your families forever?

FIRST MURDERER
We are men, my lord, (and we feel it and resent it).

MACBETH
Yes, in any list of human beings you pass for men,
just as hounds and greyhounds, mutts, spaniels, curs,

Shoughs, water-rugs and demi-wolves, are clept
95   All by the name of dogs: the valued file
Distinguishes the swift, the slow, the subtle,
The housekeeper, the hunter, every one
According to the gift which bounteous nature
Hath in him closed, whereby he does receive
100   Particular addition, from the bill
That writes them all alike: and so of men.
Now, if you have a station in the file,
Not i' th' worst rank of manhood, say 't,
And I will put that business in your bosoms
105   Whose execution takes your enemy off,
Grapples you to the heart and love of us,
Who wear our health but sickly in his life,
Which in his death were perfect.

SECOND MURDERER
                                    I am one, my liege,
Whom the vile blows and buffets of the world
110   Hath so incensed that I am reckless what
I do to spite the world.

FIRST MURDERER
                        And I another
So weary with disasters, tugged with fortune,
That I would set my life on any chance,
To mend it or be rid on 't.

MACBETH
                        Both of you
Know Banquo was your enemy.

BOTH MURDERERS
                                    True, my lord.
115
MACBETH
So is he mine, and in such bloody distance
That every minute of his being thrusts
Against my near'st of life: and though I could
With barefaced power sweep him from my sight
120   And bid my will avouch it, yet I must not,
For certain friends that are both his and mine,
Whose loves I may not drop, but wail his fall

shaggy dogs, water dogs, and half-wolves are all called
95   by the common name of "dogs." But a more detailed list
would distinguish between the fast dog, the slow, the clever,
the watchdog, the hunting dog, each one
according to the special gift with which generous nature
has endowed him. With these special qualities, he is
        distinguished by
100   his own particular title from the list
which lumps them all together. And so it is with men.
Now, if you have a special place in the list of men,
and are not the lowest of the low, speak out,
and I will tell you privately of a plot,
105   which carried out will destroy your enemy
and make you very dear to me,
whose peace of mind remains uncertain while Banquo lives,
but would become perfect if he were dead.

SECOND MURDERER
    My lord, I am a person
whom the trials and tribulations of this world
110   have so enraged that I don't care what
I do to get even with the world.

FIRST MURDERER
    And I'm another man
who is so tired of misfortunes, so yanked about by bad luck,
that I'll stake my life on any bet
either to better it or to be done with it.

MACBETH
    Both of you
now realize that Banquo was your enemy.

MURDERERS
115   We do, my lord.

MACBETH
    He is mine too ; and indeed, we are such mortal enemies
that every minute of his continuing life presses
against my heart like a dagger. And though I could
use my naked power to sweep him out of sight
120   and justify it simply by saying it is my will, yet I must not do it
because of certain mutual friends,
whose good will I can't afford to lose, but must seem to mourn

Who I myself struck down; and thence it is
That I to your assistance do make love,
125   Masking the business from the common eye
For sundry weighty reasons.

SECOND MURDERER

We shall, my lord,
Perform what you command us.

FIRST MURDERER

Though our lives—

MACBETH

Your spirits shine through you. Within this hour at most
I will advise you where to plant yourselves,
130   Acquaint you with the perfect spy o' th' time,*
The moment on 't; for 't must be done tonight,
And something from the palace; always thought
That I require a clearness: and with him—
To leave no rubs nor botches in the work—
135   Fleance his son, that keeps him company,
Whose absence is no less material to me
Than is his father's, must embrace the fate
Of that dark hour. Resolve yourselves apart:
I'll come to you anon.

MURDERERS

We are resolved, my lord.

MACBETH

140   I'll call upon you straight. Abide within.
        [*Exeunt Murderers.*]
It is concluded: Banquo, thy soul's flight,
If it find heaven, must find it out tonight.
        Exit.

Scene ii: [The palace.] Enter MACBETH's *Lady and a Servant.*

LADY MACBETH

Is Banquo gone from court?

SERVANT

Ay, madam, but returns again tonight.

---

130 *perfect . . . time* I interpret this line as "the very moment when
do it." Other editors have understood it to mean "knowledge of the exact

          the death of the very man I killed. That is why
          I have so ardently sought your help,
125   while hiding the matter from the public eye
          for various important reasons.
     SECOND MURDERER
          My lord, we'll do
          whatever you order us to.
     FIRST MURDERER
          Though our lives—
     MACBETH
          Your true spirits are showing through. Within the hour, at the
              latest,
          I'll let you know where to hide,
130   give you full information on how to do the deed,
          and the very moment when to do it, for it must be done tonight
          and at some distance from the palace. Keep in mind
          that I myself should be kept above all suspicion. And along with
              Banquo—
          to make sure of no hitches or blunders in your work—
135   his son, Fleance, who rides with him,
          whose disappearance is no less important to me
          than his father's, he too must meet the same fate
          at that dark hour. Decide by yourselves.
          I'll get back to you shortly.
     MURDERERS
          We have already decided, my lord.
     MACBETH
140   Then I'll be with you very soon. Stay inside.
              Exit Murderers.
          It is all set. Banquo, if your soul
          is going to heaven, it must discover it tonight.
              Exit MACBETH.

Act III, Scene ii: A room in Forres Castle. Enter LADY MAC-
BETH, *accompanied by a Servant.*

LADY MACBETH
     Has Banquo left the palace?
SERVANT
     Yes, madam, but he will return tonight.

---

time to do it" or as a reference to the Third Murderer.

LADY MACBETH
 Say to the King, I would attend his leisure
 For a few words.

SERVANT
     Madam, I will.
  Exit.

LADY MACBETH
        Nought's had, all's spent,
5 Where our desire is got without content:
 'Tis safer to be that which we destroy
 Than by destruction dwell in doubtful joy.
  Enter MACBETH.
 How now, my lord! Why do you keep alone,
 Of sorriest fancies your companions making,
10 Using those thoughts which should indeed have died
 With them they think on? Things without all remedy
 Should be without regard: what's done is done.

MACBETH
 We have scotched the snake, not killed it:
 She'll close and be herself, whilst our poor malice
15 Remains in danger of her former tooth.
 But let the frame of things disjoint, both the worlds suffer,
 Ere we will eat our meal in fear, and sleep
 In the affliction of these terrible dreams
 That shake us nightly. Better be with the dead,
20 Whom we, to gain our peace, have sent to peace,
 Than on the torture of the mind to lie
 In restless ecstasy. Duncan is in his grave;
 After life's fitful fever he sleeps well.
 Treason has done his worst. Nor steel, nor poison,
25 Malice domestic, foreign levy, nothing,
 Can touch him further.

LADY MACBETH
     Come on.
 Gentle my lord, sleek o'er your rugged looks;
 Be bright and jovial among your guests tonight.

LADY MACBETH
 Tell the King when he has a moment I'd like
 a few words with him.

SERVANT
 I will do so, madam.
  Exit Servant.

LADY MACBETH
 We gain nothing and sacrifice everything
5 when we get what we want without achieving happiness.
 It's better to be the victim we destroy
 than, by our act of destruction, achieve a dubious contentment.
  Enter MACBETH.
 How are you, my lord? Why do you keep to yourself,
 with such dismal reflections as your only companions,
10 living with thoughts which should have died
 with their object (i.e., Duncan)? Things that can't be changed
 should be forgotten. What's done is done.

MACBETH
 We've only wounded the snake, not killed it.
 She will heal again and be good as new, while our feeble plots
15 are still in danger of her poisonous fangs.
 But let the whole universe fall asunder, let heaven and earth
  collapse and crack apart,
 before we let ourselves eat our meals in constant fear, and sleep
 in the torment of those terrible nightmares
 that disturb us every night. Better to lie with the dead—
20 whom we sent to his peace, hoping to gain our own peace of
  mind—
 than to lie on the rack of a tortured mind
 in restless madness. Duncan is in his grave.
 After the troubled fever of life, he sleeps well.
 Treason has done its worst to him. Neither dagger, nor poison,
25 civil war, nor foreign invasion—nothing
 can harm him any more.

LADY MACBETH
 Come with me.
 My gentle lord, smooth over your troubled looks.
 Be bright and cheerful among your guests tonight.

MACBETH

So shall I, love; and so, I pray, be you.

30   Let your remembrance apply to Banquo;

Present him eminence, both with eye and tongue:

Unsafe the while, that we must lave

Our honors in these flattering streams

And make our faces vizards to our hearts,

Disguising what they are.

LADY MACBETH

35   You must leave this.

MACBETH

O, full of scorpions is my mind, dear wife!

Thou know'st that Banquo, and his Fleance, lives.

LADY MACBETH

But in them nature's copy's not eterne.

MACBETH

There's comfort yet; they are assailable.

40   Then be thou jocund. Ere the bat hath flown

His cloistered flight, ere to black Hecate's* summons

The shard-borne* beetle with his drowsy hums

Hath rung night's yawning peal, there shall be done

A deed of dreadful note.

LADY MACBETH

                        What's to be done?

MACBETH

45   Be innocent of the knowledge, dearest chuck,

Till thou applaud the deed. Come, seeling* night,

Scarf up the tender eye of pitiful day,

And with thy bloody and invisible hand

Cancel and tear to pieces that great bond*

50   Which keeps me pale! Light thickens, and the crow

Makes wing to th' rooky* wood.

Good things of day begin to droop and drowse,

Whiles night's black agents to their preys do rouse.

Thou marvel'st at my words: but hold thee still;

---

41   *Hecate*   see note at II. i. 52.

42   *shard-borne*   means either carried aloft on scaly wings or derived from and bred in dung.

46   *seeling*   in falconry to "seel" was to sew up the eyelids of a hawk to help in taming him.

MACBETH

So I shall, my love, and I beg you to do the same.
Give Banquo your full attention.
Show special consideration to him with both your looks and your
    conversation.
We are in danger as long as we have to wash
the honors that we have in streams of flattery
and make our faces masks for our hearts,
concealing what we really feel.

LADY MACBETH

You must stop thinking like this.

MACBETH

O, my conscience is full of scorpions, dear wife!
You know that Banquo and his son Fleance are both alive.

LADY MACBETH

But nature hasn't given them an eternal lease on those lives.

MACBETH

There's that comfort anyway: they are vulnerable.
Then be cheerful. Before the bat has finished
its blind flight, before black Hecate summons
the scaly-winged beetle which, with its droning,
proclaims night's sleepy presence, there will be committed
an awful and infamous crime.

LADY MACBETH

What are you going to do?

MACBETH

I don't want you to know anything about it, my pet,
until you can praise the deed (after it's done). Come, hooded
    night,
blindfold the delicate eye of the compassionate day,
and with your unseen, bloody hand
cancel and tear to pieces their (i.e., Banquo and Fleance's)
    lease on life
that frightens me into pallor. The day grows dim and the crow
    now
flies to the gloomy woods.
The wholesome creatures of day begin to nod and fall asleep,
while night's devilish agents get ready to strike at their prey.
You are amazed at my words, but don't say anything.

---

49   *bond*   cancel the obligations of loyalty and love that a king has to
his subjects and more generally that human beings have to each other.
51   *rooky wood*   a woods full of rooks, black birds about the size of
crows. Perhaps it means gloomy and smoky, with rooky derived from "roke,"
an old term for "smoke."

Things bad begun make strong themselves by ill.
So, prithee, go with me.
 Exeunt.

Scene iii: [Near the palace.] Enter Three Murderers.

FIRST MURDERER
But who did bid thee join with us?
THIRD MURDERER
       Macbeth.
SECOND MURDERER
He needs not our mistrust; since he delivers
Our offices and what we have to do
To the direction just.
FIRST MURDERER
     Then stand with us.
5 The west yet glimmers with some streaks of day.
Now spurs the lated traveler apace
To gain the timely inn, and near approaches
The subject of our watch.
THIRD MURDERER
     Hark! I hear horses.
BANQUO [*Within*]
Give us a light there, ho!
SECOND MURDERER
     Then 'tis he. The rest
10 That are within the note of expectation
Already are i' th' court.
FIRST MURDERER
     His horses go about.
THIRD MURDERER
Almost a mile: but he does usually—
So all men do—from hence to th' palace gate
Make it their walk.
SECOND MURDERER
A light, a light!
  Enter BANQUO *and* FLEANCE, *with a torch.*
THIRD MURDERER
   'Tis he.

55 Once things have begun badly, they are only strengthened by
further evil.
So, I beg you, come with me.
They exit.

Act III, Scene iii: Outside the Castle at Forres. Enter three Murderers.

FIRST MURDERER
But who asked you to join us?
THIRD MURDERER
Macbeth.
SECOND MURDERER
We can trust this fellow, since his instructions
about what we have to do
agree with what Macbeth has already told us.
FIRST MURDERER (*to Third Murderer*)
Then make a stand here with us.
5 You can still see the last rays of the sun setting in the west.
Now the delayed traveler spurs his horse
to reach his inn before dark. We should soon see the persons
we've been waiting for.
THIRD MURDERER
Listen! I hear horses.
BANQUO (*offstage, speaking to a Servant*)
Give us some light.
SECOND MURDERER
It's Banquo, then. All the
10 other guests that are expected
have already arrived.
FIRST MURDERER (*seeing that Banquo and Fleance's horses
are being led away by Servants*)
His horses are taking the long way around (to the stables).
THIRD MURDERER
That path's almost a mile long, but Banquo usually,
like everyone else, walks the rest of the way
from here to the palace gate.
SECOND MURDERER
I see a light, a light!
Enter BANQUO *and* FLEANCE, *with a torch.*
THIRD MURDERER
It's Banquo.

FIRST MURDERER

15   Stand to 't.

BANQUO

It will be rain tonight.

FIRST MURDERER

Let it come down.

[They set upon Banquo.]

BANQUO

O, treachery! Fly, good Fleance, fly, fly, fly!

[Exit FLEANCE.*]*

Thou mayst revenge. O slave!

[Dies.]

THIRD MURDERER

Who did strike out the light?

FIRST MURDERER

Was 't not the way?

THIRD MURDERER

20   There's but one down; the son is fled.

SECOND MURDERER

We have lost best half of our affair.

FIRST MURDERER

Well, let's away and say how much is done.

Exeunt.

Scene iv: [*The castle.*] *Banquet prepared. Enter* MACBETH, LADY [MACBETH], ROSS, LENNOX, *Lords, and Attendants.*

MACBETH

You know your own degrees; sit down:

At first and last, the hearty welcome.

LORDS

Thanks to your Majesty.

MACBETH

Ourself will mingle with society

5   And play the humble host.

Our hostess keeps her state, but in best time

We will require her welcome.

FIRST MURDERER
15   Hold firm, now.
BANQUO (*to Fleance*)
      It's going to rain tonight.
FIRST MURDERER
      Let the rain come down!
          They attack Banquo.
BANQUO
      Treachery! Escape, good Fleance, run, run, run!
          Exit FLEANCE *running.*
      (*Shouting to Fleance*) Avenge my death. (*To Murderer*) O
          slave! (*Dies.*)
THIRD MURDERER
      Who put out the torch?
FIRST MURDERER
      Weren't we supposed to?
THIRD MURDERER
20   We only got one of them; the son escaped.
SECOND MURDERER
      We failed in the most important part of our mission.
FIRST MURDERER
      Well, let's go to Macbeth and make our report.
          Exit Murderers.

Act III, Scene iv: The banqueting hall in Forres Castle. Enter
MACBETH *and* LADY MACBETH, *followed by* ROSS, LENNOX,
and various Lords and Attendants.

MACBETH
      You know where you're supposed to sit according to your rank;
          please sit down.
      From the noblest to the humblest, you are all most welcome.
LORDS
      Thank you, your Majesty.
MACBETH
      I'll mingle with my guests
5   and play my part as your humble host.
      My Queen will remain on the throne, but at the proper time,
      I'll ask her to welcome you too.

LADY MACBETH
Pronounce it for me, sir, to all our friends,
For my heart speaks they are welcome.
Enter First Murderer.

MACBETH
10   See, they encounter thee with their hearts' thanks.
Both sides are even: here I'll sit i' th' midst:
Be large in mirth; anon we'll drink a measure
The table round. [*Goes to Murderer*] There's blood upon thy face

MURDERER
'Tis Banquo's then.

MACBETH
15   'Tis better thee without than he within.
Is he dispatched?

MURDERER
My lord, his throat is cut; that I did for him.

MACBETH
Thou art the best o' th' cutthroats.
Yet he's good that did the like for Fleance;
20   If thou didst it, thou art the nonpareil.

MURDERER
Most royal sir, Fleance is 'scaped.

MACBETH [*Aside*]
Then comes my fit again: I had else been perfect,
Whole as the marble, founded as the rock,
As broad and general as the casing air:
25   But now I am cabined, cribbed, confined, bound in
To saucy doubts and fears.—But Banquo's safe?

MURDERER
Ay, my good lord: safe in a ditch he bides,
With twenty trenchèd gashes on his head,
The least a death to nature.

MACBETH
                              Thanks for that.
30   [*Aside*] There the grown serpent lies; the worm that's fled
Hath nature that in time will venom breed,

LADY MACBETH
Welcome all my friends for me, sir,
for in my heart I have already welcomed them.
Enter First Murderer.

MACBETH
You can see that our guests receive your greeting with heart-felt
thanks.
Since each side of the table is equal in number, I'll sit at the
head.
Enjoy yourselves fully. Soon we'll drink a toast
around the table. (*To the Murderer*) You have blood on your
face.

MURDERER
If I do, it's Banquo's.

MACBETH
Better his blood on your face than in his body.
Has he been taken care of?

MURDERER
My lord, I cut his throat—I did that much for him myself.

MACBETH
You are the best of cutthroats.
Yet whoever did the same for Fleance is a good man too.
If you did it, you are a cutthroat without equal.

MURDERER
Most royal sir, Fleance escaped.

MACBETH (*to himself*)
Then my anxiety returns. Except for this, I'd feel totally secure,
all of a piece like a marble monument, firm as a rock,
as open and free as the air that encloses us.
But now I am imprisoned, hampered, confined, hemmed in
by uncontrollable doubts and fears.—But Banquo's safe?

MURDERER
Yes, my good lord, he lies safe in a ditch
with twenty huge gashes on his head,
the smallest of which could have killed him.

MACBETH
At least I can be thankful for that.
(*To himself*) The adult snake is killed, but the young snake
that fled
has the sort of nature that will eventually produce poison,

No teeth for th' present. Get thee gone. Tomorrow
We'll hear ourselves again.
        Exit Murderer.

LADY MACBETH
                        My royal lord,
35   You do not give the cheer. The feast is sold
        That is not often vouched, while 'tis a-making,
        'Tis given with welcome. To feed were best at home;
        From thence, the sauce to meat is ceremony;
        Meeting were bare without it.
            Enter the Ghost of BANQUO, *and sits in* MACBETH'*s place.*

MACBETH
                        Sweet remembrancer!
        Now good digestion wait on appetite,
        And health on both!

LENNOX
40   May 't please your Highness sit.

MACBETH
        Here had we now our country's honor roofed,
        Were the graced person of our Banquo present—
        Who may I rather challenge for unkindness
        Than pity for mischance!

ROSS
                        His absence, sir,
45   Lays blame upon his promise. Please 't your Highness
        To grace us with your royal company?

MACBETH
        The table's full.

LENNOX
                    Here is a place reserved, sir.

MACBETH
        Where?

LENNOX
        Here, my good lord. What is 't that moves your Highness?

though he has no fangs yet. You'd better go. Tomorrow
we'll talk this matter over again.
    Exit Murderer.
LADY MACBETH
  My royal lord,
  You've not been toasting your guests. A feast is like a
    paid-for-dinner
35   . when the host does not let the guests know frequently during
    the meal
  how welcome they are. Mere eating might as well be done at
    home.
  When dining out, ceremony is the sauce for every dish;
  a social occasion is empty without it.
      Enter the Ghost of BANQUO, *and sits in Macbeth's chair*
        at the table.
MACBETH (*to Lady Macbeth*)
  Thank you for reminding me, my sweet.
  (*To his guests*) May good digestion follow good appetite,
  and may both be followed by good health!
LENNOX
40   Please sit down, your Highness.
MACBETH
  Tonight we'd have the best men in the country under one roof
  if the gracious Banquo were with us.
  I'd prefer to accuse him of thoughtlessness, rather
  than sympathize with him because he was delayed by some
    accident.
ROSS
  His absence, sir,
45   makes his promise to come seem blameworthy. But please, your
    Highness,
  will you give us the benefit of your royal presence?
MACBETH
  All the chairs are occupied.
LENNOX
  We've kept your seat for you, sir.
MACBETH
  Where?
LENNOX
  Here, my lord. What is it that upsets your Highness?

MACBETH
Which of you have done this?

LORDS
                                        What, my good lord?

50

MACBETH
Thou canst not say I did it. Never shake
Thy gory locks at me.

ROSS
Gentlemen, rise, his Highness is not well.

LADY MACBETH
Sit, worthy friends. My lord is often thus,

55   And hath been from his youth. Pray you, keep seat.
The fit is momentary; upon a thought
He will again be well. If much you note him,
You shall offend him and extend his passion.
Feed, and regard him not.—Are you a man?

MACBETH

60   Ay, and a bold one, that dare look on that
Which might appal the devil.

LADY MACBETH
                                        O proper stuff!
This is the very painting of your fear.
This is the air-drawn dagger which, you said,
Led you to Duncan. O, these flaws and starts,

65   Imposters to true fear, would well become
A woman's story at a winter's fire,
Authorized by her grandam. Shame itself!
Why do you make such faces? When all's done,
You look but on a stool.

MACBETH
                                        Prithee, see there!

70   Behold! Look! Lo! How say you?
Why, what care I? If thou canst nod, speak too.
If charnel houses* and our graves must send
Those that we bury back, our monuments
Shall be the maws of kites.
        [*Exit Ghost.*]

LADY MACBETH
                                        What, quite unmanned in folly?

---

72   *charnel houses*   houses or vaults, usually associated with a church
where dead bodies or the bones of the dead were deposited or piled up

MACBETH (*seeing the Ghost of Banquo, who is invisible to
   everyone else*)
  Which of you has done this to me?
LORDS
50   Done what, my good lord?
MACBETH (*to the Ghost*)
  You can't say I committed the murder. Don't shake
  your bloody hair at me.
ROSS
  Gentlemen, rise; his Highness is not feeling well.
LADY MACBETH
  No, stay seated, my good friends. My lord has often been like this
55 from his youth on. Please, keep seated.
  It is only a momentary fit; quick as a thought
  he'll be himself again. If you pay too much attention to him,
  you'll hurt his feelings and prolong his outburst.
  Keep eating and don't even look at him. (*To Macbeth*) Are you
   a man?
MACBETH
60 Yes, and a bold man, who dares to look on things
  that would frighten the devil.
LADY MACBETH
  What utter rubbish!
  This is a figment of your fear-ridden imagination.
  It's like the dagger hovering in the air, which you said
  led you to Duncan's bedroom. These outbursts and fits of yours
65 only pretend to express real fear. They would be more suitable
  for an old wife's tale beside a winter fireplace—
  a tale which she learned from her granny. Shame on you!
  Why do you make such faces? When all is said and done,
  you're only looking at a stool.
MACBETH
  Please, look there!
70 Do you see? Look! Observe! What do you say now?
  (*To the Ghost*) Why should I bother about you? If you can
   shake your head, you can speak too.
  If charnel houses and graves must send
  the dead back to us, our real graves
  will be in the stomachs of scavenging hawks.
    Exit Ghost.
LADY MACBETH
  Has foolish fear completely unmanned you?

Sometimes, because of lack of space, bones were taken from the graveyard
and put in a charnel house.

MACBETH
If I stand here, I saw him.
LADY MACBETH
75   Fie, for shame!
MACBETH
Blood hath been shed ere now, i' th' olden time,
Ere humane statute purged the gentle weal;
Ay, and since too, murders have been performed
Too terrible for the ear. The time has been
80   That, when the brains were out, the man would die,
And there an end; but now they rise again,
With twenty mortal murders on their crowns,
And push us from our stools. This is more strange
Than such a murder is.
LADY MACBETH
                                   My worthy lord,
Your noble friends do lack you.
MACBETH
85   I do forget.
Do not muse at me, my most worthy friends;
I have a strange infirmity, which is nothing
To those that know me. Come, love and health to all!
Then I'll sit down. Give me some wine, fill full.
          Enter Ghost.
90   I drink to th' general joy o' th' whole table,
And to our dear friend Banquo, whom we miss.
Would he were here! To all and him we thirst,
And all to all.
LORDS
                         Our duties, and the pledge.
MACBETH
95   Avaunt! and quit my sight! Let the earth hide thee!
Thy bones are marrowless, thy blood is cold;
Thou hast no speculation in those eyes
Which thou dost glare with!
LADY MACBETH
                              Think of this, good peers,
But as a thing of custom, 'tis no other.
Only it spoils the pleasure of the time.

MACBETH

As surely as I stand here now, I saw him.

LADY MACBETH

75   Shame on you!

MACBETH

Blood has been shed before this, in the olden days,

before merciful and just laws freed the state from constant
warfare.

Yes, and even after those laws were made, murders have been
committed

too terrible to hear about. In the old days

80   when a man's skull was smashed, he'd die,

and that was the end of it. But now the dead rise up again

with twenty fatal wounds on their heads

and push us out of our stools. This is stranger

than the murder itself.

LADY MACBETH

My worthy lord,

your noble guests miss you at table.

MACBETH

85   I had forgotten them.

(*To his guests*) Don't be amazed at me, my dearest friends.

I have a peculiar illness, which is not even worth noticing

by those who know me well. Come, I'll propose a toast of love
and health to all;

then I'll sit down. Give me some wine; fill the cup to the brim.

Enter the Ghost of BANQUO.

90   I drink to the joy of everyone at this table

and to our dear friend Banquo, whom we miss.

I wish he were here! I drink to Banquo and to all of you

and let everybody drink to everybody else.

LORDS

We pledge our loyalty and good faith to you.

MACBETH(*seeing the Ghost*)

Get out! Leave my sight! Bury yourself in the earth!

95   Your bones are without any marrow; your blood is cold;

you have no perception in those eyes

you glare at me with!

LADY MACBETH (*to the Guests*)

Consider this, my friends,

as a recurring condition; it's nothing special.

I apologize, though, because it spoils the evening's pleasure.

MACBETH

100   What man dare, I dare.
Approach thou like the rugged Russian bear,
The armed rhinoceros, or th' Hyrcan* tiger;
Take any shape but that, and my firm nerves
Shall never tremble. Or be alive again,
105   And dare me to the desert with thy sword.
If trembling I inhabit then, protest me
The baby of a girl. Hence, horrible shadow!
Unreal mock'ry, hence!
        [*Exit Ghost.*]
                            Why, so: being gone,
I am a man again—Pray you, sit still.

LADY MACBETH

110   You have displaced the mirth, broke the good meeting,
With most admired disorder.

MACBETH

                            Can such things be,
And overcome us like a summer's cloud,
Without our special wonder? You make me strange
Even to the disposition that I owe,
115   When now I think you can behold such sights,
And keep the natural ruby of your cheeks,
When mine is blanched with fear.

ROSS

                            What sights, my lord?

LADY MACBETH

I pray you, speak not: he grows worse and worse;
Question enrages him: at once, good night.
120   Stand not upon the order of your going,
But go at once.

LENNOX

                Good night; and better health
Attend his Majesty!

LADY MACBETH

                    A kind good night to all!
        Exeunt Lords.

---

102   *Hyrcan*   from Hyrcania, an ancient region south of the Caspian Sea
and reported by Pliny to be a place where tigers were bred.

MACBETH (*to the Ghost*)

100   I'll dare what any man dares.
If you would approach me in the shape of the huge Russian bear,
the armored rhinoceros, the Hyrcanian tiger—
take any shape you wish except that of Banquo and my sinews
would never tremble. Or come back to life again
105   and challenge me to fight with swords in some lonely place.
If I tremble then, you can call me
the puny baby of a young girl. Away you hideous ghost!
Unreal and mocking illusion, get out of here!
      Exit Ghost.
So—it is gone
and I am a man again. (*To the Guests*) Please don't get up.

LADY MACBETH (*to Macbeth*)

110   You have spoiled our pleasure and broken up this friendly
       gathering
with your most surprising and disruptive behavior.

MACBETH

Can things like this exist
and can we let them pass over us like a summer cloud
without being utterly amazed? You make me unsure
of what kind of man I really am
115   when, it occurs to me, you can see such sights
and still keep the natural redness of your cheeks
while mine are absolutely white with fear.

ROSS

What sights, my lord?

LADY MACBETH

I beg you, don't speak about it any further. He grows worse
      and worse.
Questioning infuriates him. Let me wish you a quick good night.
120   Don't bother about the formalities of leave-taking,
but just go right away.

LENNOX

Good night. I hope his Majesty will
soon be feeling better.

LADY MACBETH

A warm good night to all!
      Exit Lords.

MACBETH

It will have blood, they say: blood will have blood.
Stones have been known to move and trees to speak;
125   Augures and understood relations have
By maggot-pies and choughs and rooks brought forth
The secret'st man of blood. What is the night?

LADY MACBETH

Almost at odds with morning, which is which.

MACBETH

How say'st thou, that Macduff denies his person
At our great bidding?

LADY MACBETH
                              Did you send to him, sir?
130

MACBETH

I hear it by the way, but I will send.
There's not a one of them but in his house
I keep a servant fee'd. I will tomorrow,
And betimes I will, to the Weird Sisters:
135   More shall they speak, for now I am bent to know
By the worst means, the worst. For mine own good
All causes shall give way. I am in blood
Stepped in so far that, should I wade no more,
Returning were as tedious as go o'er.
140   Strange things I have in head that will to hand,
Which must be acted ere they may be scanned.

LADY MACBETH

You lack the season of all natures, sleep.

MACBETH

Come, we'll to sleep. My strange and self-abuse
Is the initiate fear that wants hard use.
145   We are yet but young in deed.
                    Exeunt.

MACBETH

> The murdered will have vengeance, they say; blood must be paid
> for with blood.
> Stones have been known to move and trees to speak.

125
> Seers, by piecing together all the facts
> and by studying the flights of magpies, crows, and rooks, have
> discovered
> the best-concealed killer. What time of night is it?

LADY MACBETH

> It's almost dawn, neither night nor day.

MACBETH

> What do you think of Macduff's refusal to come to our feast,
> though he received our personal invitation?

LADY MACBETH

130
> Did you send a message to him, sir?

MACBETH

> I've heard Macduff's absence commented on, incidentally, but I
> will send for information.
> There's not one lord's house
> where I don't have a paid servant to spy for me. Tomorrow
> morning,
> and early too, I will go to the Witches.

135
> I will get them to tell me more, because I am determined to know
> the worst no matter what it takes. For my own good,
> I won't let anything stand in my way. I have waded into the
> river of blood
> so far, that even if I go no farther,
> it would be as tiring to go back as to proceed to the other side.

140
> I have strange plans in my head that demand execution,
> and I must do them before I have a chance to think too much
> about them.

LADY MACBETH

> What you need is something that helps everyone: the refresh-
> ment of a good night's sleep.

MACBETH

> Come, let's go to sleep. My strange self-deception
> is only the fear of a beginner who's not yet experienced in
> evil-doing.
> We are still new to this business.
> > *They exit.*

Scene v: [A Witches' haunt.] Thunder. Enter the Three Witches, meeting HECATE.

FIRST WITCH

  Why, how now, Hecate! you look angerly.

HECATE

  Have I not reason, beldams as you are,
  Saucy and overbold? How did you dare
  To trade and traffic with Macbeth
  In riddles and affairs of death;
  And I, the mistress of your charms,
  The close contriver of all harms,
  Was never called to bear my part,
  Or show the glory of our art?

10 And, which is worse, all you have done
  Hath been but for a wayward son,
  Spiteful and wrathful, who, as others do,
  Lives for his own ends, not for you.
  But make amends now: get you gone

15 And at the pit of Acheron*
  Meet me i' th' morning. Thither he
  Will come to know his destiny.
  Your vessels and your spells provide,
  Your charms and everything beside.

20 I am for th' air; this night I'll spend
  Unto a dismal and a fatal end:
  Great business must be wrought ere noon.
  Upon the corner of the moon
  There hangs a vap'rous drop profound;

25 I'll catch it ere it come to ground:
  And that distilled by magic sleights
  Shall raise such artificial sprites
  As by the strength of their illusion
  Shall draw him on to his confusion.

30 He shall spurn fate, scorn death, and bear
  His hopes 'bove wisdom, grace, and fear:
  And you all know security
  Is mortals' chiefest enemy.
          Music and a song.

---

15 *pit of Acheron* perhaps this is a reference to the Scottish cavern
where the Witches assemble in Act IV, scene i. Properly, Acheron is the
name of a river in Hades.

Act III, Scene v: A barren heath. Thunder. Enter the Three Witches, meeting HECATE.

FIRST WITCH
Why, what's the matter, Hecate? You look angry.

HECATE
Why shouldn't I, since you hags
are so impertinent and bold. How dare you
bargain and trade with Macbeth
5   in mysteries and matters of death?
Why wasn't I, the mistress of your magic spells,
the secret planner of all mischief,
ever called upon to play my role
or demonstrate the glory of our magic?
10   And what is even worse, you have done all this
for an irresponsible man, one who is
both angry and spiteful, and who, like other men,
works only for his own ends, not yours.
But you can correct this now. Go quickly,
15   and at the pit of Acheron
meet me in the morning. There, Macbeth
will come to find out his fate.
Bring your equipment and your spells,
your charms and everything else.
20   I must fly away. I'll spend tonight
plotting a foreboding and fatal purpose.
I've got a great deal to do before noon.
From a corner of the moon
hangs a heavy drop of moisture.
25   I'll catch it before it hits the ground
and that drop, distilled by my magical powers,
will conjure up spirits so unnatural
that by their deluding powers
they'll lure him to his destruction.
30   He will reject fate, scorn death, and maintain
his hopes beyond all wisdom, virtue, and fear.
As you know, over-confidence
is man's mortal enemy.
      Music is heard and a song.

Hark! I am called; my little spirit, see,
35   Sits in a foggy cloud and stays for me.
                [*Exit.*]

FIRST WITCH
    Come, let's make haste; she'll soon be back again.
        Exeunt.

Scene vi: [The palace.] Enter LENNOX *and another Lord.*

LENNOX
    My former speeches have but hit your thoughts,
    Which can interpret farther. Only I say
    Things have been strangely borne. The gracious Duncan
    Was pitied of Macbeth: marry, he was dead.
5   And the right-valiant Banquo walked too late;
    Whom, you may say, if 't please you, Fleance killed,
    For Fleance fled. Men must not walk too late.
    Who cannot want the thought, how monstrous
    It was for Malcolm and for Donalbain
10   To kill their gracious father? Damnèd fact!
    How it did grieve Macbeth! Did he not straight,
    In pious rage, the two delinquents tear,
    That were the slaves of drink and thralls of sleep?
    Was not that nobly done? Ay, and wisely too;
15   For 'twould have angered any heart alive
    To hear the men deny 't. So that I say
    He has borne all things well: and I do think
    That, had he Duncan's sons under his key—
    As, an 't please heaven, he shall not—they should find
20   What 'twere to kill a father. So should Fleance.
    But, peace! for from broad words, and 'cause he failed
    His presence at the tyrant's feast, I hear,
    Macduff lives in disgrace. Sir, can you tell
    Where he bestows himself?

Listen! I am being called. See, my attendant spirit
35   sits in a misty cloud waiting for me.
       Exit HECATE.

FIRST WITCH
     Come, let's hurry. She'll soon be back again.
       They exit.

Act III, Scene vi: Outside the Castle at Forres. Enter LENNOX
and another Lord.

LENNOX (*ironically*)
     My earlier remarks, then, go along with what you've been
        thinking and
     you can draw your own conclusions. I must say, though,
     that things have been oddly managed. Kindly King Duncan
     was pitied by Macbeth: and rightly so, because he is now dead.
5   And the brave Banquo stayed out too late.
     You can, if you like, say his son Fleance killed him,
     because Fleance fled. Men ought not to go out for a walk too late
        at night.
     Who can fail to think how vicious
     it was of Malcolm and Donalbain
10   to kill their kindly father. A damnable crime!
     How it saddened Macbeth! Didn't he immediately,
     in his holy anger, kill those delinquent guards,
     while they were dead drunk and fast asleep?
     Wasn't that nobly done? Yes, and wisely too,
15   for it would have enraged any living person
     to hear those two deny their guilt. Therefore, I tell you
     Macbeth has managed everything very nicely. I think
     that if he had Duncan's sons under lock and key—
     and I hope to God he never does—they'd find out
20   what happens to those who kill their father. Fleance would too.
     But enough! Because of speaking so broadly (as I do), and
        because he failed
     to show up at the tyrant's feast, I hear that
     Macduff is in disgrace. Sir, can you tell me
     where he's keeping himself?

LORD

                          The son of Duncan,

25   From whom this tyrant holds the due of birth,

Lives in the English court, and is received

Of the most pious Edward* with such grace

That the malevolence of fortune nothing

Takes from his high respect. Thither Macduff

30   Is gone to pray the holy King, upon his aid

To wake Northumberland and warlike Siward,*

That by the help of these, with Him above

To ratify the work, we may again

Give to our tables meat, sleep to our nights,

35   Free from our feasts and banquets bloody knives,

Do faithful homage and receive free honors:

All which we pine for now. And this report

Hath so exasperate the King that he

Prepares for some attempt of war.

LENNOX

                         Sent he to Macduff?

LORD

40   He did: and with an absolute "Sir, not I,"

The cloudy messenger turns me his back

And hums, as who should say "You'll rue the time

That clogs me with this answer."

LENNOX

                      And that well might

Advise him to a caution, t' hold what distance

45   His wisdom can provide. Some holy angel

Fly to the court of England and unfold

His message ere he come, that a swift blessing

May soon return to this our suffering country

Under a hand accursed!

LORD

                   I'll send my prayers with him.

        Exeunt.

---

27 *Edward* Edward the Confessor, King of England 1042-66.

LORD

Malcolm, the son of King Duncan,

25   who is denied his royal birthright by this tyrant,

lives at the English court. He is welcomed

so graciously by the devout King Edward,

that in spite of Malcolm's bad luck,

this King still has great respect for him. Macduff is on his way there

30   to beg this holy King to help him

rouse Northumberland and the fierce Siward.

With their help, and with God above

to bless the mission, we may once again

bring food to our tables and sleep to our nightly beds,

35   free our feasts and banquets from bloody knives,

pledge our loyalty, and receive honors with no strings attached—

all of which we long for now. And this report

has so exasperated Macbeth that he

is getting ready for war.

LENNOX

Did he send to Macduff (i.e., for support)?

LORD

40   He did, but Macduff answered with an unambiguous "Sir, not I."

The sullen messenger turned his back on him

and whistled a tune, as if to say, "You'll regret

burdening me with such an answer (for Macbeth)!"

LENNOX

And that ought to

warn Macduff to be cautious and keep as much distance

45   (from Macbeth) as his good sense can provide. May some holy angel

fly to the English court and present Macduff's

plea before he gets there, so that a swift blessing

may soon return to our country, suffering

under this damned tyrant's hand!

LORD

My prayers go with him.

    They exit.

---

31 *Siward* Earl of Northumberland.

Act IV, Scene i: [A Witches' haunt.] Thunder. Enter the Three Witches.

FIRST WITCH
Thrice the brinded cat hath mewed.
SECOND WITCH
Thrice and once the hedge-pig whined.
THIRD WITCH
Harpier* cries. 'Tis time, 'tis time.
FIRST WITCH
Round about the cauldron go:
5   In the poisoned entrails throw.
Toad, that under cold stone
Days and nights has thirty-one
Swelt'red venom sleeping got,
Boil thou first i' th' charmèd pot.
ALL
10   Double, double toil and trouble;
Fire burn and cauldron bubble.
SECOND WITCH
Fillet of a fenny snake,
In the cauldron boil and bake;
Eye of newt and toe of frog,
15   Wool of bat and tongue of dog,
Adder's fork and blindworm's* sting,
Lizard's leg and howlet's wing,
For a charm of pow'rful trouble,
Like a hell-broth boil and bubble.
ALL
20   Double, double toil and trouble;
Fire burn and cauldron bubble.
THIRD WITCH
Scale of dragon, tooth of wolf,
Witch's mummy, maw and gulf
Of the ravined salt-sea shark,
25   Root of hemlock digged i' th' dark,
Liver of blaspheming Jew,
Gall of goat, and slips of yew
Slivered in the moon's eclipse,

---

3 *Harpier* the "familiar" of the Third Witch. See notes at I. i. 8-9.

Act IV, Scene i: A barren heath. Thunder. Enter Three Witches.

FIRST WITCH
  The streaked cat has meowed three times.

SECOND WITCH
  The hedgehog has whined three times and once more.

THIRD WITCH
  My spirit, Harpier, cries, "It's time, it's time."

FIRST WITCH
  Dance around the kettle.
5 Throw in the poisoned guts.
  Let the toad—who, under a cold stone
  for thirty-one days and nights,
  has been sweating poison while sleeping—
  boil first in the magic pot.

ALL
10 Double, double toil and trouble;
  fire burn and kettle bubble.

SECOND WITCH
  Throw a slice of swamp-snake
  into the boiling kettle and let it cook,
  then the eye of a salamander, the toe of a frog,
15 bat's fur, dog's tongue,
  serpent's forked tongue and poisoned worms,
  lizard's leg and owl's wing,
  all of these to make a spell of powerful mischief,
  so boil and bubble like a hellish soup.

ALL
20 Double, double toil and trouble;
  fire burn and kettle bubble.

THIRD WITCH
  Throw in a dragon's scale, a wolf's fang,
  a bit of mummified witch, the stomach and gullet
  of the ravenous ocean shark,
25 poisoned-hemlock root dug up in the night,
  the liver of a God-insulting Jew,
  goat's bile, and yew twigs
  snipped off during the moon's eclipse,

---

16 *blindworm* a harmless kind of legless lizard, but thought to be
poisonous in Elizabethan times.

Nose of Turk and Tartar's lips,
30   Finger of birth-strangled babe
Ditch-delivered by a drab,
Make the gruel thick and slab:
Add thereto a tiger's chaudron,
For th' ingredients of our cauldron.

ALL
35   Double, double toil and trouble;
Fire burn and cauldron bubble.

SECOND WITCH
Cool it with a baboon's blood,
Then the charm is firm and good.
          Enter HECATE *and the other Three Witches.*

HECATE
O, well done! I commend your pains;
40   And every one shall share i' th' gains:
And now about the cauldron sing,
Like elves and fairies in a ring,
Enchanting all that you put in.
          Music and a song: "Black Spirits" &c.*
          [*Exeunt* HECATE *and the other Three Witches.*]

SECOND WITCH
By the pricking of my thumbs,
45   Something wicked this way comes:
          [*Knocking.*]
Open, locks,
Whoever knocks!
          Enter MACBETH.

MACBETH
How now, you secret, black, and midnight hags!
What is 't you do?

ALL
                    A deed without a name.

MACBETH
50   I conjure you, by that which you profess,
Howe'er you come to know it, answer me:
Though you untie the winds and let them fight
Against the churches; though the yeasty waves

---

43 *Black Spirits* The text of a song beginning in this way appears in
Thomas Middleton's *The Witch* (V, ii), but there it is sung by the son of

Turk's nose and Tartar's lips,
30   finger of a baby strangled at birth and
born from a whore in a ditch.
Make the soup thick and heavy.
Add also a tiger's gizzards
to the ingredients of our kettle.

ALL
35   Double, double toil and trouble;
fire burn and kettle bubble.

SECOND WITCH
Cool it with a baboon's blood
to make the spell strong and effective.
    Enter HECATE *with three other witches.*

HECATE
Ah, well done! I compliment you on your work,
40   and every one will share in the profits.
And now let's sing around the kettle
like elves and fairies in a circle,
bewitching everything you put in.
    Music and a song are heard from offstage.
    Exit HECATE *and the three other witches.*

SECOND WITCH
I know by the way my thumbs are tingling
45   that something wicked is coming this way.
    Knocking.
Open, locks, to
whoever knocks!
    Enter MACBETH.

MACBETH
So here you are, you mysterious, black hags of midnight!
What are you up to?

ALL
What we do has no name.

MACBETH
50   I demand of you, by the black arts you practice—
however you came by the knowledge—answer me.
Though you release the winds and let them storm
against the churches, though the foaming waves

Hecate. Actually this song, as the one in *Macbeth,* III, vi, is irrelevant to
Shakespeare's play and may have been added for entertainment.

Confound and swallow navigation up;
55   Though bladed corn be lodged and trees blown down;
Though castles topple on their warders' heads;
Though palaces and pyramids do slope
Their heads to their foundations; though the treasure
Of nature's germens* tumble all together,
60   Even till destruction sicken,* answer me
To what I ask you.

FIRST WITCH

Speak.

SECOND WITCH

Demand.

THIRD WITCH

We'll answer.

FIRST WITCH
Say, if th' hadst rather hear it from our mouths,
Or from our masters?

MACBETH

Call 'em, let me see 'em.

FIRST WITCH
Pour in sow's blood, that hath eaten
65   Her nine farrow; grease that's sweaten
From the murderer's giblet throw
Into the flame.

ALL

Come, high or low,
Thyself and office deftly show!
Thunder. First Apparition: an Armed Head.

MACBETH
Tell me, thou unknown power——

FIRST WITCH

70   He knows thy thought:
Hear his speech, but say thou nought.

FIRST APPARITION
Macbeth! Macbeth! Macbeth! Beware Macduff!
Beware the Thane of Fife. Dismiss me: enough.
He descends.

---

59   *nature's germens*   the accumulated store of those elemental seeds
or germs from which everything in the future is to spring.

55 shipwreck and swallow up ships at sea,
though ripe corn be beaten flat and trees blown down,
though castles topple on their keepers' heads,
though the tops of palaces and pyramids are bent
over to their foundations, though the irreplaceable
60 seeds of all being are allowed to be jumbled together
until no less than the destruction of all life is threatened,
  I demand
what I ask you.

FIRST WITCH
Speak.

SECOND WITCH
Demand.

THIRD WITCH
We'll answer.

FIRST WITCH
Tell us if you would rather hear the answers from our own
  mouths
or from our masters?

MACBETH
Call your masters; I want to see them.

FIRST WITCH
Pour into the kettle the blood of a pig that has eaten
65 her own litter of nine; and throw the grease that oozes
from the murderer's gallows
into the flames.

ALL
From on high or from below,
show yourselves and skillfully display your function.
  Thunder. The First Illusion appears: A Helmeted Head.

MACBETH
Tell me, you unknown power—

FIRST WITCH
He knows your thoughts.
70 Just listen to what he says and keep quiet.

FIRST ILLUSION
Macbeth! Macbeth! Macbeth! Beware of Macduff,
who is the Thane of Fife! Let me go. I've said enough.
  He disappears through a trap-door in the stage.

---

60   *sicken*   is satiated and becomes sick at the sight of its own work.

MACBETH
Whate'er thou art, for thy good caution thanks:
Thou hast harped my fear aright. But one word more——

FIRST WITCH
75   He will not be commanded. Here's another,
More potent than the first.
          Thunder. Second Apparition: a Bloody Child.

SECOND APPARITION
Macbeth! Macbeth! Macbeth!

MACBETH
Had I three ears, I'd hear thee.

SECOND APPARITION
80   Be bloody, bold, and resolute! Laugh to scorn
The power of man, for none of woman born
Shall harm Macbeth.
          Descends.

MACBETH
Then live, Macduff: what need I fear of thee?
But yet I'll make assurance double sure,
And take a bond of fate. Thou shalt not live;
85   That I may tell pale-hearted fear it lies,
And sleep in spite of thunder.
          Thunder. Third Apparition: a Child Crowned, with a tree in
          his hand.
                              What is this,
That rises like the issue of a king,
And wears upon his baby-brow the round
And top of sovereignty?

ALL
                    Listen, but speak not to 't.

THIRD APPARITION
90   Be lion-mettled, proud, and take no care
Who chafes, who frets, or where conspirers are:
Macbeth shall never vanquished be until
Great Birnam Wood to high Dunsinane Hill
Shall come against him.
          Descends.

MACBETH
> I thank you—whatever you are—for your helpful warning.
> You've played the very tune of my fear. Just one more word—

75 FIRST WITCH
> He will not take orders. Here comes another,
> more powerful than the first.
>> *Thunder. The Second Illusion appears: A Bloody Child.*

SECOND ILLUSION
> Macbeth! Macbeth! Macbeth!

MACBETH
> If I had three ears, I couldn't hear you better.

SECOND ILLUSION
> Be violent, bold, and determined! Laugh scornfully
80 > at the power of man, for no man born of woman
> can harm Macbeth.
>> *He disappears through a trap-door.*

MACBETH
> I'll let you live then, Macduff. Why should I fear you?
> But wait, I'll make doubly sure
85 > and bind Fate to a contract. You shall not live, Macduff.
> Then I can tell my cowardly fear that it lies,
> and I can sleep in spite of the turmoil around me.
>> *Thunder. The Third Illusion appears: A Crowned Child*
>> *with a branch in his hand.*
> What illusion is this,
> that arises looking like a King's son,
> and on his infant head wears the circle
> and crown of royal power?

ALL
> Listen, but don't speak to it.

90 THIRD ILLUSION
> Be fierce as a lion, be proud, and don't worry about
> who is angry, who is irritated, or where secret plotters might be.
> Macbeth will never be conquered until
> great Birnam Wood to high Dunsinane Hill
> marches against him.
>> *He disappears through a trap-door.*

MACBETH
                              That will never be.
95   Who can impress the forest, bid the tree
       Unfix his earth-bound root? Sweet bodements, good!
       Rebellious head, rise never, till the Wood
       Of Birnam rise, and our high-placed Macbeth
       Shall live the lease of nature, pay his breath
100   To time and mortal custom. Yet my heart
       Throbs to know one thing. Tell me, if your art
       Can tell so much: shall Banquo's issue ever
       Reign in his kingdom?
ALL
                              Seek to know no more.
MACBETH
       I will be satisfied. Deny me this,
105   And an eternal curse fall on you! Let me know.
       Why sinks that cauldron? And what noise is this?
                Hautboys.
FIRST WITCH
       Show!
SECOND WITCH
       Show!
THIRD WITCH
       Show!
ALL
110   Show his eyes, and grieve his heart;
       Come like shadows, so depart!
                A show of eight Kings and BANQUO, *last* [*King*] *with a glass*
                in his hand.
MACBETH
       Thou art too like the spirit of Banquo. Down!
       Thy crown does sear mine eyeballs. And thy hair,
       Thou other gold-bound brow, is like the first.
115   A third is like the former. Filthy hags!
       Why do you show me this? A fourth! Start, eyes!
       What, will the line stretch out to th' crack of doom?
       Another yet! A seventh! I'll see no more.
       And yet the eighth appears, who bears a glass
120   Which shows me many more; and some I see

MACBETH

95   That will never happen.
Who can enlist the forest, order a tree
to uproot itself from its fixed place in the earth? These are
   wonderful predictions! Good!
An armed force of rebels will never rise against me until
100   Birnam Wood revolts too, and our exalted Macbeth
shall live out his alloted years, breathing calmly,
day by day, until his natural death. Yet my heart
craves to know one thing. Tell me—if your powers
can tell this much—will Banquo's children ever
rule in this kingdom?

ALL

   Ask no more questions.

MACBETH

105   I want to know everything. Deny me this answer
and may you be cursed for all eternity! I must know.
Why is the kettle disappearing? What music do I hear?
   Oboes are heard from offstage.

FIRST WITCH

   Show him!

SECOND WITCH

   Show him!

THIRD WITCH

   Show him!

110 ALL

   Let him see and break his heart.
Come and go like shadows.
   Enter the Ghost of BANQUO, *followed by a procession of*
   eight Kings, the last with a mirror in his hand.

MACBETH

   You look too much like the spirit of Banquo. Vanish!
Your crown burns my eyeballs. And your hair,
115   you second gold-crowned head, is like the first.
And the third one is just like the second. Filthy hags!
Why are you showing me this? A fourth! My eyes are popping!
What! Will the line of Kings stretch out to doomsday?
And yet another! Now a seventh! I'll see no more.
120   And now the eighth appears, and he carries a mirror
which shows me many more kings. I see some

That twofold balls and treble scepters* carry:
Horrible sight! Now I see 'tis true;
For the blood-boltered Banquo smiles upon me,
And points at them for his. What, is this so?

FIRST WITCH
125   Ay, sir, all this is so. But why
Stands Macbeth thus amazedly?
Come, sisters, cheer we up his sprites,
And show the best of our delights:
I'll charm the air to give a sound,
130   While you perform your antic round,
That this great king may kindly say
Our duties did his welcome pay.
            Music. The Witches dance, and vanish.

MACBETH
Where are they? Gone? Let this pernicious hour
Stand aye accursèd in the calendar!
Come in, without there!
            Enter LENNOX.

LENNOX
135   What's your Grace's will?

MACBETH
Saw you the Weird Sisters?

LENNOX
                    No, my lord.

MACBETH
Came they not by you?

LENNOX
                    No, indeed, my lord.

MACBETH
Infected be the air whereon they ride,
And damned all those that trust them! I did hear
140   The galloping of horse. Who was 't came by?

LENNOX
'Tis two or three, my lord, that bring you word
Macduff is fled to England.

MACBETH
                    Fled to England?

---

121   *twofold balls and treble scepters*   the balls are usually taken to
refer to the double coronation of James I in Scotland and in England. The
treble scepters are the two used for investment in the English coronation,

special royal insignia: the two-fold ball and triple scepter.
O terrible sight! Now I see that the prediction is true,
because the blood-covered ghost of Banquo smiles at me,
and points to those kings as his own offspring. What, is that
    the way it is?

FIRST WITCH

125   Yes, sir, just so. But why,
Macbeth, do you stand there so stunned?
Come, sisters, let's cheer up his spirits;
we'll show him our best number.
I'll bewitch the air into making music,

130   while you perform your strange dance,
so that Macbeth will graciously admit
that our attentions made him feel welcome.
    Music. The Witches dance and then vanish.

MACBETH

Where are they? Have they gone? Let this evil hour
be forever marked on the calendar as accursed.
    (*To Lennox, offstage*) You out there, come in!
    Enter LENNOX.

LENNOX

135   What do you wish, sir?

MACBETH

Did you see the Three Witches?

LENNOX

No, my lord.

MACBETH

Didn't they pass by you?

LENNOX

Definitely not, my lord.

MACBETH

Let the air they ride on be contagious,
and let all who trust them be damned. I heard

140   horses galloping. Who was it that came by?

LENNOX

It was two or three riders, my lord, who came to tell you
that Macduff has fled to England.

MACBETH

Fled to England?

---

and the one used in the Scottish coronation. The passage is clearly a tribute
to James I and the union of Great Britain under him.

LENNOX
Ay, my good lord.

MACBETH [*Aside*]
Time, thou anticipat'st my dread exploits.
145 The flighty purpose never is o'ertook
Unless the deed go with it. From this moment
The very firstlings of my heart shall be
The firstlings of my hand. And even now,
To crown my thoughts with acts, be it thought and done:
150 The castle of Macduff I will surprise;
Seize upon Fife; give to th' edge o' th' sword
His wife, his babes, and all unfortunate souls
That trace him in his line. No boasting like a fool;
This deed I'll do before this purpose cool:
155 But no more sights!—Where are these gentlemen?
Come, bring me where they are.
     Exeunt.

Scene ii: [MACDUFF's *castle.*] *Enter* MACDUFF's *wife, her Son, and* ROSS.

LADY MACDUFF
What had he done, to make him fly the land?

ROSS
You must have patience, madam.

LADY MACDUFF
                     He had none:
His flight was madness. When our actions do not,
Our fears do make us traitors.

ROSS
                    You know not
5 Whether it was his wisdom or his fear.

LADY MACDUFF
Wisdom! To leave his wife, to leave his babes,
His mansion and his titles, in a place
From whence himself does fly? He loves us not;
He wants the natural touch: for the poor wren,
10 The most diminutive of birds, will fight,

LENNOX
  Yes, my good lord.

MACBETH (*to himself*)
  Time, you foresee my dreadful deeds.
145 A quickly conceived plan is never fulfilled
  unless the deed follows right after the thought. From now on
  the immediate impulses of my heart will be
  followed by the immediate actions of my hand. And even now,
  to cap these thoughts with actions, let this thought be
    accomplished:
150 I will take the castle of Macduff by surprise.
  I will seize Macduff's property in Fife, put to the sword
  his wife, his children, and all those unfortunate creatures
  who are related to him. But I will not boast like a fool.
  I'll do the deed before my intention cools.
155 But let me see no more illusions!—Where are these messengers?
  Come, bring me to them.
    They exit.

Act IV, Scene ii: Macduff's castle at Fife. Enter LADY MAC-
DUFF, *her Son, and* ROSS.

LADY MACDUFF
  What reason did my husband have for fleeing from Scotland?

ROSS
  Please be patient, madam.

LADY MACDUFF
  What patience did he have?
  His fleeing was insane. Even when our actions are not traitorous,
  our fear can make us look like traitors.

ROSS
  You don't know
5 whether it was his wisdom or his fear that made him leave.

LADY MACDUFF
  Wisdom! What kind of wisdom is it to leave his wife, his
    children,
  his castle, and his possessions, and to leave them in a place
  from which he himself runs in fear? He doesn't love us.
  He has no normal, protective instincts; even the poor wren,
10 the tiniest of birds, will fight,

Her young ones in her nest, against the owl.
All is the fear and nothing is the love;
As little is the wisdom, where the flight
So runs against all reason.

ROSS
                              My dearest coz,
15   I pray you, school yourself. But, for your husband,
He is noble, wise, judicious, and best knows
The fits o' th' season. I dare not speak much further:
But cruel are the times, when we are traitors
And do not know ourselves; when we hold rumor
20   From what we fear yet know not what we fear,
But float upon a wild and violent sea
Each way and move. I take my leave of you.
Shall not be long but I'll be here again.
Things at the worst will cease, or else climb upward
25   To what they were before. My pretty cousin,
Blessing upon you!

LADY MACDUFF
Fathered he is, and yet he's fatherless.

ROSS
    I am so much a fool, should I stay longer,
It would be my disgrace and your discomfort.
I take my leave at once.
        Exit Ross.

LADY MACDUFF
30   Sirrah, your father's dead:
And what will you do now? How will you live?

SON
    As birds do, mother.

LADY MACDUFF
                          What, with worms and flies?

SON
    With what I get, I mean; and so do they.

LADY MACDUFF
    Poor bird! thou'dst never fear the net nor lime,*
35   The pitfall nor the gin.

---

34 *lime* birdlime, a sticky substance smeared on tree branches to catch
small birds.

when her fledglings are in the nest, against the owl.
Macduff acted entirely out of fear; there was no love in it.
And there was no wisdom in it either, since his flight
goes against all reason.

ROSS

My dearest kinswoman,
15   I beg you, get hold of yourself. As for your husband,
he is noble, wise, level-headed, and he knows best
how the wind is blowing. I dare not say much more.
But these are dangerous times when we are judged traitors
without even knowing it ourselves; when we believe rumors
20   because we are afraid, and yet we don't know what it is we fear,
but we are adrift on a wild and violent sea,
tossed about in all directions. I must leave now.
It won't be long before I'll return.
Things this bad can't get any worse, or else they may bounce
     back
25   to what they were before. (*Turning to Macduff's son*) My
     handsome kinsman,
God be with you.

LADY MACDUFF

He has a father and yet he's fatherless.

ROSS

I'm such a sentimental fool that if I stay any longer
I'll disgrace myself (i.e., by weeping) and embarrass you.
I'm leaving right now.
     Exit ROSS.

LADY MACDUFF
30   Since, my lad, your father's dead,
what will you do now? How will you live?

SON

As birds do, mother.

LADY MACDUFF

What! Will we feed ourselves on worms and flies?

SON

I mean we'll live on what I can find, just like the birds.

LADY MACDUFF

My poor bird! Wouldn't you be afraid of being captured
     by net or bird-lime,
35   trap or snare?

SON
  Why should I, mother? Poor birds they are not set for.
  My father is not dead, for all your saying.
LADY MACDUFF
  Yes, he is dead: how wilt thou do for a father?
SON
  Nay, how will you do for a husband?
LADY MACDUFF
40 Why, I can buy me twenty at any market.
SON
  Then you'll buy 'em to sell again.
LADY MACDUFF
  Thou speak'st with all thy wit, and yet, i' faith,
  With wit enough for thee.
SON
  Was my father a traitor, mother?
LADY MACDUFF
45 Ay, that he was.
SON
  What is a traitor?
LADY MACDUFF
  Why, one that swears and lies.
SON
  And be all traitors that do so?
LADY MACDUFF
  Every one that does so is a traitor, and must be hanged.
SON
50 And must they all be hanged that swear and lie?
LADY MACDUFF
  Every one.
SON
  Who must hang them?
LADY MACDUFF
  Why, the honest men.
SON
  Then the liars and swearers are fools; for there are liars and
55 swearers enow to beat the honest men and hang up them.
LADY MACDUFF
  Now, God help thee, poor monkey! But how wilt thou do for a
  father?

SON
Why should I, mother? Nobody sets traps for ordinary birds.
Besides, in spite of what you say, my father is not dead.
LADY MACDUFF
Yes he is dead. What are you going to do for a father?
SON
Well, what will you do for a husband?
LADY MACDUFF
40   Why, I can buy myself twenty of them at any market.
SON
Then you're buying them only to sell them again.
LADY MACDUFF
Your wisdom is rather childish and yet I must admit
it's witty enough for a child.
SON
Was my father a traitor, mother?
LADY MACDUFF
45   Yes, he was.
SON
What is a traitor?
LADY MACDUFF
Why, it is a person who swears to an oath and then breaks it
by lying.
SON
Anyone who does that is a traitor?
LADY MACDUFF
Yes, anyone who does so is a traitor and must be hanged.
SON
50   You really mean that everyone who swears and lies must be
hanged?
LADY MACDUFF
Everyone.
SON
Who has to hang them?
LADY MACDUFF
Why the honest men.
SON
Then the liars and swearers are fools, for there
55   are enough of them to beat up the honest men and hang them.
LADY MACDUFF
Now, God help you, my poor little monkey! But
what are you going to do for a father?

SON
  If he were dead, you'd weep for him. If you would not, it were a
  good sign that I should quickly have a new father.
LADY MACDUFF
60   Poor prattler, how thou talk'st!
        Enter a Messenger.
MESSENGER
  Bless you, fair dame! I am not to you known,
  Though in your state of honor I am perfect.
  I doubt some danger does approach you nearly:
  If you will take a homely man's advice,
65   Be not found here; hence, with your little ones.
  To fright you thus, methinks I am too savage;
  To do worse to you were fell cruelty,
  Which is too nigh your person. Heaven preserve you!
  I dare abide no longer.
        Exit Messenger.
LADY MACDUFF
                    Whither should I fly?
70   I have done no harm. But I remember now
  I am in this earthly world, where to do harm
  Is often laudable, to do good sometime
  Accounted dangerous folly. Why then, alas,
  Do I put up that womanly defense,
75   To say I have done no harm?—What are these faces?
        Enter Murderers.
MURDERER
  Where is your husband?
LADY MACDUFF
  I hope, in no place so unsanctified
  Where such as thou mayst find him.
MURDERER
                    He's a traitor.
SON
  Thou li'st, thou shag-haired villain!
MURDERER
                    What, you egg!
        [*Stabbing him.*]
  Young fry of treachery!

SON

    If he were really dead, you'd weep for him. If you

    didn't weep at his death, it would be a good sign that I'd soon

      have a new father.

LADY MACDUFF

60   Poor little chatterer, how you do talk!

      Enter a Messenger.

MESSENGER

    Bless you, good lady. You don't know me,

    though I am fully aware of your honorable rank.

    I'm afraid that some danger is approaching very close to you.

    If you will take a plain man's advice,

65   don't be found here; go away and take your little ones with you.

    I feel I am being brutal to frighten you this way,

    but it would be an even greater cruelty not to warn you

    of the danger which is already too near. May heaven protect you.

      Exit Messenger.

LADY MACDUFF

    Where should I flee to?

70   I have done nothing wrong. But I remember now

    that I am in a corrupt world, where to do harm

    is often praised and to do good is sometimes

    considered dangerous folly. Why then, alas,

    do I still rely on my woman's defense

75   by saying that I have done nothing wrong?—Whose faces are

      these I see?

      Enter Murderers.

MURDERER

    Where's your husband?

LADY MACDUFF

    I hope he's not in a place so godless

    that men like you might find him.

MURDERER

    He's a traitor.

SON

    You're a liar, you shaggy-haired villain!

MURDERER

    Why you brat!

      The Murderer stabs him.

    Little upstart of a traitor!

80 SON
                    He has killed me, mother:
        Run away, I pray you!
            [*Dies.*]
            Exit [LADY MACDUFF], *crying "Murder!"* [*followed by
            Murderers*].

Scene iii: [*England. Before the King's palace.*] *Enter* MALCOLM
and MACDUFF.

MALCOLM
        Let us seek out some desolate shade, and there
        Weep our sad bosoms empty.
MACDUFF
                        Let us rather
        Hold fast the mortal sword, and like good men
5   Bestride our down-fall'n birthdom. Each new morn
        New widows howl, new orphans cry, new sorrows
        Strike heaven on the face, that it resounds
        As if it felt with Scotland and yelled out
        Like syllable of dolor.
MALCOLM
                        What I believe, I'll wail;
10   What know, believe; and what I can redress,
        As I shall find the time to friend, I will.
        What you have spoke, it may be so perchance.
        This tyrant, whose sole name blisters our tongues,
        Was once thought honest: you have loved him well;
15   He hath not touched you yet. I am young; but something
        You may deserve of him through me, and wisdom
        To offer up a weak, poor, innocent lamb
        T' appease an angry god.
MACDUFF
        I am not treacherous.
MALCOLM
                        But Macbeth is.
20   A good and virtuous nature may recoil
        In an imperial charge. But I shall crave your pardon;
        That which you are, my thoughts cannot transpose:

SON
80　　He has killed me, mother.
　　　Run away, I beg you!
　　　　　The son dies.
　　　　　Exit LADY MACDUFF *running and crying "Murder!,"*
　　　　　followed by the Murderers.

Act IV, Scene iii: England. Before the King's palace. Enter
MALCOLM *and* MACDUFF.

MALCOLM
　　　Let's find a solitary spot in the woods and
　　　cry our sad hearts out there.
MACDUFF
　　　I'd rather
　　　take up our deadly swords, and like the good men we are,
　　　stand guard over our prostrate native land. Every morning
5　　　new widows howl, new orphans cry, new sorrows
　　　slap high heaven on the face, so that heaven echoes as if it were
　　　in sympathy with Scotland and shouted out
　　　the same sounds of pain.
MALCOLM
　　　What I can believe in these reports, I'll grieve about,
　　　but I only believe what I know for a fact. What I can remedy,
10　　　when the time is right, I will.
　　　Perhaps what you report is true.
　　　This tyrant, Macbeth, whose very name blisters our tongues,
　　　was once thought a good man. You were his good friend,
　　　so he hasn't touched you yet. Even though I'm young, you may
　　　　　gain something
15　　　by turning me over to him, and you might think it wise
　　　to offer me up as a weak, poor, innocent lamb (i.e., a sacrifice)
　　　to appease an angry god (i.e., Macbeth).
MACDUFF
　　　I'm not a double-crosser.
MALCOLM
　　　But Macbeth is.
　　　A good, decent nature can give way
20　　　under pressure from a king. But I beg your pardon.
　　　Whatever your nature is cannot be changed by what I think
　　　　　of you.

Angels are bright still, though the brightest fell:
Though all things foul would wear the brows of grace,
Yet grace must still look so.

MACDUFF

I have lost my hopes.

MALCOLM

25   Perchance even there where I did find my doubts.
Why in that rawness left you wife and child,
Those precious motives, those strong knots of love,
Without leave-taking? I pray you,
Let not my jealousies be your dishonors,
30   But mine own safeties. You may be rightly just
Whatever I shall think.

MACDUFF

Bleed, bleed, poor country!
Great tryranny, lay thou thy basis sure,
For goodness dare not check thee: wear thou thy wrongs;
The title is affeered. Fare thee well, lord:
35   I would not be the villain that thou think'st
For the whole space that's in the tyrant's grasp
And the rich East to boot.

MALCOLM

Be not offended;
I speak not as in absolute fear of you.
I think our country sinks beneath the yoke;
40   It weeps, it bleeds, and each new day a gash
Is added to her wounds. I think withal
There would be hands uplifted in my right;
And here from gracious England have I offer
Of goodly thousands. But, for all this,
45   When I shall tread upon the tyrant's head,
Or wear it on my sword, yet my poor country
Shall have more vices than it had before,
More suffer, and more sundry ways than ever,
By him that shall succeed.

Angels are still luminous though Lucifer, most resplendent of
them all, fell.
Though all evil things would like to look virtuous,
only virtue can look like virtue.

MACDUFF
I have lost all hope (i.e., of gaining your trust).

MALCOLM
25
Maybe you lost your hopes in the same place I discovered my
doubts.
Why did you leave so unprotected your wife and children—
those priceless reasons for living, those firm ties of love—
without so much as saying good-bye? I beg you,
don't let my suspicions seem like reflections on your honor,
but take them only as precautions I must use for my own safety.
30
You may be a perfectly honorable man,
whatever thoughts I have about you.

MACDUFF
Bleed, bleed, my unfortunate country!
Monstrous tyranny, you can construct a firm foundation,
because good men are afraid to stop you ; display your crimes
openly,
for your claim is legally sanctioned. Good-bye, sir.
35
I'd never be the villain you take me for,
not for the whole kingdom ruled by that tyrant,
not even if you threw in the riches of the East as well.

MALCOLM
Don't be offended.
I'm not so absolutely fearful of you.
I think our country is sinking underneath the burden of its
slavery.
40
It weeps, it bleeds, and every new day another gash
is added to her wounds. Besides, I think
I can get support for my claim to the throne.
Right here, I have offers from the noble King of England
of many thousands of soldiers. But in spite of this,
45
when I put my foot on this tyrant's head,
or carry it stuck on my sword, my poor country still
will have more vices than it had before.
It will suffer more, and in more ways than it ever had before,
at the hands of Macbeth's successor.

MACDUFF

What should he be?

MALCOLM

50   It is myself I mean; in whom I know
All the particulars of vice so grafted
That, when they shall be opened, black Macbeth
Will seem as pure as snow, and the poor state
Esteem him as a lamb, being compared
With my confineless harms.

MACDUFF

55   Not in the legions
Of horrid hell can come a devil more damned
In evils to top Macbeth.

MALCOLM

I grant him bloody,
Luxurious, avaricious, false, deceitful,
Sudden, malicious, smacking of every sin
60   That has a name: but there's no bottom, none,
In my voluptuousness: your wives, your daughters,
Your matrons and your maids, could not fill up
The cistern of my lust, and my desire
All continent impediments would o'erbear,
65   That did oppose my will. Better Macbeth
Than such an one to reign.

MACDUFF

Boundless intemperance
In nature is a tyranny; it hath been
Th' untimely emptying of the happy throne,
And fall of many kings. But fear not yet
70   To take upon you what is yours: you may
Convey your pleasures in a spacious plenty,
And yet seem cold, the time you may so hoodwink.
We have willing dames enough. There cannot be
That vulture in you, to devour so many
75   As will to greatness dedicate themselves,
Finding it so inclined.

MALCOLM

With this there grows
In my most ill-composed affection such

MACDUFF
Who is the successor to be?

MALCOLM
50   I mean myself. I recognize in myself
all the various details of evil so grafted to my nature
that when they shall be exposed, black-hearted Macbeth
will seem as pure as snow, and poor Scotland
will consider him a lamb when they compare his doings
with my limitless crimes.

MACDUFF
55   Not in all the armies
of dreadful hell is there a devil so damnable
as to outdo Macbeth in evil.

MALCOLM
I admit he is murderous,
lustful, greedy, lying, deceitful,
violent, hateful, tainted with every sin
60   that has a name. But there is absolutely no satisfying
my lust: your wives, your daughters,
women young and old, could not fill up
the huge vessel of my lust. My desires
would overcome all restraining obstacles
65   that got in my way. Better to have Macbeth
ruling than someone like myself.

MACDUFF
Unlimited lust
in a man's nature is a tyrant. It's been the cause
of a prosperous reign's sudden end
and the downfall of many kings. But don't be afraid in advance
70   to accept what is yours. You can
discreetly carry on plenty of affairs
and yet appear so cold that you can fool everybody.
We have enough women who are willing. Your lust cannot be
so vulture-like as to swallow up all the women
75   willing to submit themselves to a king,
when they find he desires them.

MALCOLM
Together with my lust, there grows
in my unbalanced character such

A stanchless avarice that, were I King,
I should cut off the nobles for their lands,
80   Desire his jewels and this other's house:
And my more-having would be as a sauce
To make me hunger more, than I should forge
Quarrels unjust against the good and loyal,
Destroying them for wealth.

MACDUFF
                              This avarice
85   Sticks deeper, grows with more pernicious root
Than summer-seeming lust, and it hath been
The sword of our slain kings. Yet do not fear.
Scotland hath foisons to fill up your will
Of your mere own. All these are portable,
90   With other graces weighed.

MALCOLM
But I have none. The king-becoming graces,
As justice, verity, temp'rance, stableness,
Bounty, perseverance, mercy, lowliness,
Devotion, patience, courage, fortitude,
95   I have no relish of them, but abound
In the division of each several crime,
Acting it many ways. Nay, had I pow'r, I should
Pour the sweet milk of concord into hell,
Uproar the universal peace, confound
All unity on earth.

MACDUFF
100   O Scotland, Scotland!

MALCOLM
If such a one be fit to govern, speak:
I am as I have spoken.

MACDUFF
                        Fit to govern!
No, not to live. O nation miserable!
With an untitled tyrant bloody-sceptered,
105   When shalt thou see thy wholesome days again,
Since that the truest issue of thy throne
By his own interdiction stands accursed,

an insatiable greed that, if I were king,
I'd get rid of my noble followers only to seize their lands—
80   I would want this one's jewels and that one's castle—
and what I acquired would only whet
my appetite for more, so that I would trump up
unjust quarrels against my worthy and loyal followers
just so that I could destroy them for their wealth.

MACDUFF
Such greed
85   sinks deeper and grows more dangerous roots
than lust, that only is appropriate for the summer of life, and
    greed has been
the killer of many of our slain kings. Still have no fear;
Scotland has resources enough to satisfy your greed
entirely out of what will be yours. These vices are bearable
90   when balanced against your many virtues.

MALCOLM
But I have none. Virtues proper to a king,
such as justice, truthfulness, self-control, stability,
generosity, perseverance, mercy, humility,
loyalty, patience, courage, endurance—
95   I have no taste for them. Rather, my mind is filled
with the different forms of each type of crime
and the various ways to commit them. No, if I had a king's power
    I would
pour the sweet milk of harmony into hell,
throw the general peace into confusion, and destroy
all unity on earth.

MACDUFF
100   O Scotland, Scotland!

MALCOLM
Tell me if such a person is fit to rule Scotland;
I am the kind of man I've described.

MACDUFF
Fit to rule!
No! You're not fit to live. O wretched country!
Ruled by an illegitimate tyrant, holding a bloody scepter!
105   When will you see happy days again,
since the rightful heir to the throne
stands condemned by his own judgment

134   *Macbeth*

And does blaspheme his breed? The royal father
Was a most sainted king : the queen that bore thee,
110   Oft'ner upon her knees than on her feet,
Died every day she lived. Fare thee well!
These evils thou repeat'st upon thyself
Hath banished me from Scotland. O my breast,
Thy hope ends here!

MALCOLM
                              Macduff, this noble passion,
115   Child of integrity, hath from my soul
Wiped the black scruples, reconciled my thoughts
To thy good truth and honor. Devilish Macbeth
By many of these trains hath sought to win me
Into his power; and modest wisdom plucks me
120   From over-credulous haste: but God above
Deal between thee and me! For even now
I put myself to thy direction, and
Unspeak mine own detraction; here abjure
The taints and blames I laid upon myself,
125   For strangers to my nature. I am yet
Unknown to woman, never was forsworn,
Scarcely have coveted what was mine own,
At no time broke my faith, would not betray
The devil to his fellow, and delight
130   No less in truth than life. My first false speaking
Was this upon myself. What I am truly,
Is thine and my poor country's to command.
Whither indeed, before thy here-approach,
Old Siward, with ten thousand warlike men,
135   Already at a point was setting forth.
Now we'll together, and the chance of goodness
Be like our warranted quarrel! Why are you silent?

MACDUFF
Such welcome and unwelcome things at once
'Tis hard to reconcile.
          Enter a Doctor.

and slanders his own heritage? Your royal father, Duncan,
was a most saintly king. The queen who gave you birth
110   spent more time praying on her knees than walking on her feet,
and died (to this world) every day she lived. Good-bye.
These vices you have confessed to
have banished me from Scotland (i.e., because you will never
    reconquer it). O my heart!
With this, your last hope is gone.

MALCOLM

Macduff, your noble anguish
115   born of your integrity has, from my soul,
erased all dark suspicions and convinced me
of your sound honesty and honor. Fiendish Macbeth
has used a number of lures, trying to entice me
into his power. So far prudent caution has rescued me
from being too trusting and making hasty moves. But may
120   God above
oversee our dealings! For right now
I put myself in your hands, and
take back the harsh things I said about myself. I here renounce
the evils and faults I accused myself of
125   as being alien to my nature. I am still a
virgin, never committed perjury,
hardly wanted to possess my own things,
never broke a promise, would not betray
one devil to another, and find as much pleasure
130   in truth as in life itself. The first lies I ever spoke
were those I just told against myself. My true self
is at your service, and at the service of our pitiable country.
In fact, just before you arrived, it was toward Scotland
that old Siward, with ten thousand warriors
135   ready for battle, was going.
Now we'll go there together. May the chance of our success
be equal to the justice of our cause! Why are you silent?

MACDUFF

I find such good and bad news coming at the same time
hard to deal with.
    Enter a Doctor.

MALCOLM

140   Well, more anon. Comes the King forth, I pray you?

DOCTOR

Ay, sir. There are a crew of wretched souls
That stay his cure: their malady* convinces
The great assay of art; but at his touch,
Such sanctity hath heaven given his hand,
They presently amend.

MALCOLM

                    I thank you, doctor.
145
        Exit [Doctor].

MACDUFF

What's the disease he means?

MALCOLM

                    'Tis called the evil:
A most miraculous work in this good King,
Which often since my here-remain in England
I have seen him do. How he solicits heaven,
150   Himself best knows: but strangely-visited people,
All swoll'n and ulcerous, pitiful to the eye,
The mere despair of surgery, he cures,
Hanging a golden stamp about their necks,
Put on with holy prayers: and 'tis spoken,
155   To the succeeding royalty he leaves
The healing benediction. With this strange virtue
He hath a heavenly gift of prophecy,
And sundry blessings hang about his throne
That speak him full of grace.
        Enter ROSS.

MACDUFF

                    See, who comes here?

MALCOLM

160   My countryman; but yet I know him not.

MACDUFF

My ever gentle cousin, welcome hither.

MALCOLM

I know him now: good God, betimes remove
The means that makes us strangers!

---

142 *their malady* "the King's Evil," scrofula, frequently characterized
by an enlarged degeneration of lymphatic glands in the neck. The disease

MALCOLM

40 Well, we'll talk more about it soon. (*To the Doctor*) Please, can
you tell me if the King's coming out?

DOCTOR

Yes sir. There's a crowd of miserable creatures
waiting for him to cure them. Their sickness defeats
all efforts of medical science, but at his touch—
such holiness has heaven given to his hand—
they recover immediately.

MALCOLM

45 Thank you, Doctor.
Exit Doctor.

MACDUFF

What disease is he talking about?

MALCOLM

It's called "the king's evil."
The good King has an absolutely miraculous power
which often, since I've been here in England,
I have seen him use. How he moves heaven

50 he himself only knows, but strangely diseased people,
all swollen and ulcerous, pathetic to look at,
the utter despair of surgery, he cures,
and he hangs a gold medal around their necks,
put on while reciting holy prayers. They say

55 he will pass on to the kings who follow him
this blessed healing power. Together with this wonderful skill,
he also has the holy gift of foreseeing the future,
and many other blessings hover near his throne
that proclaim him full of holiness.
Enter ROSS.

MACDUFF

Look who is coming here.

MALCOLM

60 He's from Scotland, but I don't know him.

MACDUFF

Welcome to England, my most noble kinsman.

MALCOLM

I recognize him now. Good God, may we quickly be free
from the obstacles that keep us separated from each other.

---

was thought to be curable at the touch of any king descended from Edward,
the Confessor.

ROSS

                            Sir, amen.

MACDUFF

    Stands Scotland where it did?

ROSS

                        Alas, poor country!

165   Almost afraid to know itself! It cannot
    Be called our mother but our grave, where nothing
    But who knows nothing is once seen to smile;
    Where sighs and groans, and shrieks that rent the air,
    Are made, not marked; where violent sorrow seems
170   A modern ecstasy. The dead man's knell
    Is there scarce asked for who, and good men's lives
    Expire before the flowers in their caps,
    Dying or ere they sicken.

MACDUFF

                    O, relation

    Too nice, and yet too true!

MALCOLM

                  What's the newest grief?

ROSS

175   That of an hour's age doth hiss the speaker;
    Each minute teems a new one.

MACDUFF

                  How does my wife?

ROSS

    Why, well.

MACDUFF

    And all my children?

ROSS

                  Well too.

MACDUFF

    The tyrant has not battered at their peace?

ROSS

    No; they were well at peace when I did leave 'em.

MACDUFF

180   Be not a niggard of your speech: how goes 't?

ROSS

    When I came hither to transport the tidings,
    Which I have heavily borne, there ran a rumor

ROSS
May it be so, sir.

MACDUFF
Is Scotland still in the same situation?

ROSS
Alas, the miserable country!
65   It is almost afraid to know what's happened to it! It can't
be called our mother, but rather our grave, a place where no one
ever smiles except those ignorant of what is going on;
a place where the sighs, groans, and shrieks that fill the air
are sounded but go unnoticed, where extreme sorrow seems like
70   a routine emotion. The bell tolling for the dead
hardly prompts people to ask for whom it tolls, and good men
die before the flowers in their caps wither,
dying before they have a chance to get sick.

MACDUFF
O, your report
is too exact, and yet too true!

MALCOLM
What's the most recent sorrow?

ROSS
75   Any report an hour old gets the speaker hissed off the stage—
each minute produces a new cause for grief.

MACDUFF
How is my wife?

ROSS
Why, well.

MACDUFF
And all my children?

ROSS
Well too.

MACDUFF
The tyrant has not hacked at their peaceful existence?

ROSS
No. They were certainly at peace when I left them.

MACDUFF
80   Don't be stingy with your words. What's going on?

ROSS
On my way here with the news,
which I've brought with much sadness, I heard a rumor

Of many worthy fellows that were out;
Which was to my belief witnessed the rather,
185 For that I saw the tyrant's power afoot.
Now is the time of help. Your eye in Scotland
Would create soldiers, make our women fight,
To doff their dire distresses.

MALCOLM
                                        Be 't their comfort
We are coming thither. Gracious England hath
190 Lent us good Siward and ten thousand men;
An older and a better soldier none
That Christendom gives out.

ROSS
                                        Would I could answer
This comfort with the like! But I have words
That would be howled out in the desert air,
Where hearing should not latch them.

MACDUFF
195   What concern they?
The general cause or is it a fee-grief
Due to some single breast?

ROSS
                                        No mind that's honest
But in it shares some woe, though the main part
Pertains to you alone.

MACDUFF
                                        If it be mine,
200 Keep it not from me, quickly let me have it.

ROSS
Let not your ears despise my tongue for ever,
Which shall possess them with the heaviest sound
That ever yet they heard.

MACDUFF
                                        Humh! I guess at it.

ROSS
Your castle is surprised; your wife and babes
205 Savagely slaughtered. To relate the manner,
Were, on the quarry of these murdered deer,
To add the death of you.

about many first-rate soldiers ready for battle,
which was confirmed for me all the more
185　when I saw Macbeth's troops stirring.
Now is the time for you to come and help. Your presence in
　　Scotland
would enlist soldiers and make even our women fight
to rid themselves of their frightful troubles.

MALCOLM
Let them take heart;
we are on our way there. The gracious King of England has
190　lent us ten thousand soldiers and good Siward;
there is no more experienced or better soldier
in all Christendom (i.e., Europe).

ROSS
I wish I could
match this good news. But I have news
that should be howled out in the desert
where no one could hear it.

MACDUFF
195　What is it about?
Does it concern the nation, or is it a particular sorrow,
belonging to a single heart?

ROSS
No honest mind
can help but share in this sorrow, but the main part
pertains to you alone.

MACDUFF
Since it's mine,
200　don't keep it from me. Tell me quickly.

ROSS
Don't hate me forever for what I'm going to say.
I'm about to inform you of the saddest news
that you have ever heard.

MACDUFF
Well, I can guess at it.

ROSS
Your castle was attacked without warning. Your wife and
　　children
205　were savagely murdered. To give you the details
would, in the face of this pile of slaughtered dear ones,
kill you too.

MALCOLM

                              Merciful heaven!
What, man! Ne'er pull your hat upon your brows;
Give sorrow words. The grief that does not speak
210   Whispers the o'er-fraught heart, and bids it break.

MACDUFF

   My children too?

ROSS

                     Wife, children, servants, all
That could be found.

MACDUFF

                      And I must be from thence!
My wife killed too?

ROSS

               I have said.

MALCOLM

                        Be comforted.
Let's make us med'cines of our great revenge,
215   To cure this deadly grief.

MACDUFF

   He has no children. All my pretty ones?
Did you say all? O hell-kite! All?
What, all my pretty chickens and their dam
At one fell swoop?

MALCOLM

   Dispute it like a man.

MACDUFF

220   I shall do so;
But I must also feel it as a man.
I cannot but remember such things were,
That were most precious to me. Did heaven look on,
And would not take their part? Sinful Macduff,
225   They were all struck for thee! Naught that I am,
Not for their own demerits but for mine
Fell slaughter on their souls. Heaven rest them now!

MALCOLM

   Be this the whetstone of your sword. Let grief
Convert to anger; blunt not the heart, enrage it.

MALCOLM
  Merciful heaven!
  (*To Macduff*) What are you doing, man? Don't pull your
    hat over
  your eyes, but speak about your sorrow. The grief that is
    unexpressed
210 whispers to the overburdened heart and tells it to break.
MACDUFF
  My children too?
ROSS
  Wife, children, servants, everyone
  that could be found.
MACDUFF
  And I had to be away from home!
  My wife killed too?
ROSS
  I told you.
MALCOLM
  There is one consolation.
  Our great revenge can become the medicine
215 to cure this deadly grief.
MACDUFF
  Macbeth has no children. All my pretty children?
  Did you say all? O hell-hawk! All?
  Can it be! All my pretty babes and their mother killed
  in one deadly swoop?
MALCOLM
  Avenge it like a man.
MACDUFF
220 I shall do so,
  but first I must feel my loss as a man.
  I cannot help remembering the existence of those
  who were so dear to me. Could heaven watch
  and not fight for them? Sinful Macduff!
225 They were all killed because of you! I'm the wicked one.
  It was not for their faults, but for mine
  that they were slaughtered. Now, may heaven grant them peace!
MALCOLM
  May your sorrow be the sharpening stone for your sword.
    Let your grief
  turn to anger. Don't calm your rage but feed it full.

MACDUFF

230   O, I could play the woman with mine eyes,
And braggart with my tongue! But, gentle heavens,
Cut short all intermission; front to front
Bring thou this fiend of Scotland and myself;
Within my sword's length set him. If he 'scape,
Heaven forgive him too!

MALCOLM

235   This tune goes manly.
Come, go we to the King. Our power is ready;
Our lack is nothing but our leave. Macbeth
Is ripe for shaking, and the powers above
Put on their instruments. Receive what cheer you may.
240   The night is long that never finds the day.
        Exeunt.

Act V, Scene i: [Dunsinane. In the castle.] Enter a Doctor of Physic and a Waiting-Gentlewoman.

DOCTOR

I have two nights watched with you, but can perceive no truth in your report. When was it she last walked?

GENTLEWOMAN

Since his Majesty went into the field, I have seen her rise from her bed, throw her nightgown upon her, unlock her closet, take
5   forth paper, fold it, write upon 't, read it, afterwards seal it, and again return to bed; yet all this while in a most fast sleep.

DOCTOR

A great perturbation in nature, to receive at once the benefit of sleep and do the effects of watching! In this slumb'ry agitation, besides her walking and other actual performances, what, at any
10   time, have you heard her say?

GENTLEWOMAN

That, sir, which I will not report after her.

DOCTOR

You may to me, and 'tis most meet you should.

MACDUFF

Oh, I could act like a woman with my eyes (i.e., weep)
and brag with my tongue! But merciful heaven,
shorten the time until I meet Macbeth;
bring this fiend of Scotland and myself face to face;
only bring him within range of my sword. If he escape me,
let heaven forgive him too.

MALCOLM

This is a manly tune.
Come, let's go to the English King. Our army is ready;
we only need to say good-bye. Macbeth
is ripe to be shaken from his throne, and the heavenly powers
urge us on as their agents. Be as cheerful as you can.
Even the longest night is followed by the day.
They exit.

*Act V, Scene i: A room in Macbeth's castle at Dunsinane. Enter a
Doctor and one of the Queen's Ladies-in-Waiting.*

DOCTOR

I have stayed up with you for two nights, but haven't seen
   anything to confirm
your report. When did you last see her walking in her sleep?

LADY

She's been doing it ever since the King went to the battlefield.
   I have seen her get out of
bed, put on her dressing gown, open her desk, take
out paper, fold it, write on it, read it, and then seal it and
again return to her bed; and all the while she is fast asleep.

DOCTOR

It's a serious disturbance in natural function to enjoy at the
   same time the relaxation of
sleep and to act like a person awake. While she's sleep-walking,
aside from the walking and other physical actions, what
have you heard her speak at any time?

LADY

That, sir, which I won't repeat after her.

DOCTOR

You may tell me and it's perfectly proper for you to do so.

GENTLEWOMAN
   Neither to you nor anyone, having no witness to confirm my
   speech.

   Enter LADY [MACBETH], *with a taper.*

15 Lo you, here she comes! This is her very guise, and, upon my
   life, fast asleep! Observe her; stand close.

DOCTOR
   How came she by that light?

GENTLEWOMAN
   Why, it stood by her. She has light by her continually. 'Tis her
   command.

DOCTOR
20 You see, her eyes are open.

GENTLEWOMAN
   Ay, but their sense is shut.

DOCTOR
   What is it she does now? Look, how she rubs her hands.

GENTLEWOMAN
   It is an accustomed action with her, to seem thus washing her
   hands: I have known her continue in this a quarter of an hour.

LADY MACBETH
25 Yet here's a spot.

DOCTOR
   Hark! she speaks. I will set down what comes from her, to satisfy
   my remembrance the more strongly.

LADY MACBETH
   Out, damned spot! Out, I say! One: two: why, then 'tis time to
   do 't. Hell is murky. Fie, my lord, fie! A soldier, and afeard?
30 What need we fear who knows it, when none can call our pow'r
   to accompt? Yet who would have thought the old man to have
   had so much blood in him?

DOCTOR
   Do you mark that?

LADY MACBETH
   The Thane of Fife had a wife. Where is she now? What, will

LADY

I'm not going to tell you or anyone else, since there is no witness
to verify my report.

Enter LADY MACBETH, *with a lighted candle.*

But look, here she comes! Just as she usually does and, as sure as
15   I'm breathing, she's fast asleep! Watch her, but keep out of
sight.

DOCTOR

Where did she get the candle?

LADY

Why, it was near her bed. She always has some light near her;
it's her order.

DOCTOR

Notice that her eyes are open.

LADY

20   Yes, but they have no ability to perceive anything.

DOCTOR

What is she doing now? Look, how she rubs her hands.

LADY

It's a habit with her to seem to be washing her
hands like that. I have known her to keep it up for a quarter of
an hour.

LADY MACBETH

Still here's a stain.

DOCTOR

25   Listen! She's speaking. I will write down what she says to make
sure of my memory.

LADY MACBETH

Out, damned spot! Wash out, I say! (*Seems to hear a bell.*) One,
two. Why then it's time to
do the murder. Hell is dark and obscure. (*Speaking to Macbeth*)
Can you be a soldier and still be afraid?
Why should we care who knows about it, when no one dare
question our actions
30   and call us to account? And yet who would have thought the
old man (i.e., Duncan)
had so much blood in him?

DOCTOR

Did you hear that?

LADY MACBETH

Macduff, the Thane of Fife, had a wife. Where is she now?
What, will

35 these hands ne'er be clean? No more o' that, my lord, no more o' that! You mar all with this starting.

DOCTOR
Go to, go to! You have known what you should not.

GENTLEWOMAN
She has spoke what she should not, I am sure of that. Heaven knows what she has known.

LADY MACBETH
40 Here's the smell of the blood still. All the perfumes of Arabia will not sweeten this little hand. Oh, oh, oh!

DOCTOR
What a sigh is there! The heart is sorely charged.

GENTLEWOMAN
I would not have such a heart in my bosom for the dignity of the whole body.

DOCTOR
45 Well, well, well——

GENTLEWOMAN
Pray God it be, sir.

DOCTOR
This disease is beyond my practice. Yet I have known those which have walked in their sleep who have died holily in their beds.

LADY MACBETH
50 Wash your hands; put on your nightgown; look not so pale! I tell you yet again, Banquo's buried. He cannot come out on 's grave.

DOCTOR
Even so?

LADY MACBETH
To bed, to bed! There's knocking at the gate. Come, come, come, come, give me your hand! What's done cannot be undone. To 55 bed, to bed, to bed!

Exit LADY [MACBETH].

DOCTOR
Will she go now to bed?

GENTLEWOMAN
Directly.

I never be able to clean these hands? (*To Macbeth*) Stop it,
my lord,

35   stop it! You'll ruin everything with your nervousness.
DOCTOR
Come, come! You've heard what you should not hear.
LADY
I'm certain that she has said what she should not say.
Only heaven
knows what she knows.
LADY MACBETH
I can still smell the blood. All the perfumes of Arabia will

40   not make this little hand sweet again. Oh, Oh, Oh!
DOCTOR
What a sigh that was! Her heart is extremely burdened.
LADY
I wouldn't have such a heart in my breast for all the nobility of
the rest of her person.
DOCTOR
Well, well, well—
LADY

45   I pray to God that all will be well, sir.
DOCTOR
This illness is beyond my medical skill. Nevertheless, I've known
sleep-walkers who have died piously in their
beds.
LADY MACBETH (*to Macbeth*)
Wash your hands. Put on your nightgown. Don't look so pale!
Again, I tell

50   you that Banquo's buried. He can't rise from his grave.
DOCTOR
That too?
LADY MACBETH (*to Macbeth*)
Go to bed, to bed! Someone's knocking at the gate. Come with
me, come, come,
come! Give me your hand! What's done cannot be undone. To
bed, to bed, to bed!
LADY MACBETH exits.
DOCTOR

55   Will she go to bed now?
LADY
Immediately.

DOCTOR

    Foul whisp'rings are abroad. Unnatural deeds
    Do breed unnatural troubles. Infected minds
60   To their deaf pillows will discharge their secrets.
    More needs she the divine than the physician.
    God, God forgive us all! Look after her;
    Remove from her the means of all annoyance,
    And still keep eyes upon her. So good night.
65   My mind she has mated and amazed my sight:
    I think, but dare not speak.

GENTLEWOMAN

                  Good night, good doctor.

    Exeunt.

Scene ii: [*The country near Dunsinane.*] *Drum and colors. Enter*
MENTEITH, CAITHNESS, ANGUS, LENNOX, *Soldiers.*

MENTEITH

    The English power is near, led on by Malcolm,
    His uncle Siward and the good Macduff.
    Revenges burn in them; for their dear causes
    Would to the bleeding and the grim alarm
    Excite the mortified man.

ANGUS

5   Near Birnam Wood
    Shall we well meet them; that way are they coming.

CAITHNESS

    Who knows if Donalbain be with his brother?

LENNOX

    For certain, sir, he is not. I have a file
    Of all the gentry. There is Siward's son,
10   And many unrough youths that even now
    Protest their first of manhood.

MENTEITH

                  What does the tyrant?

CAITHNESS

    Great Dunsinane he strongly fortifies.
    Some say he's mad; others, that lesser hate him,
    Do call it valiant fury: but, for certain,

DOCTOR

Ugly rumors are flying about. Abnormal actions
can produce abnormal disturbances. Those with tainted minds
will confess their secrets to their deaf pillows.
60   She has more need of a priest than a doctor.
God, God forgive us all! Take care of her;
take anything dangerous away from her;
and keep a constant eye on her. So good night.
She's baffled my mind and bewildered my eyes.
65   I have opinions but don't dare say a word.

LADY

Good night, good doctor.
They exit.

*Act V, Scene ii: A field near Macbeth's castle at Dunsinane. Drums
and flags. Enter* MENTEITH, CAITHNESS, ANGUS, LENNOX,
and Soldiers.

MENTEITH

The English army is nearby, led by Malcolm,
his uncle Siward, and the good Macduff.
They are burning for revenge. Their deeply felt motives
would call even a dead man to bloody and
terrifying battle.

ANGUS

5   Near Birnam Wood
we shall easily meet them. That's the way they are coming.

CAITHNESS

Does anyone know if Donalbain is with his brother Malcolm?

LENNOX

I'm quite sure he's not, sir. I have a list
of all the nobility. Siward's son is on the list
10   and many beardless young men who right now (i.e., in this battle)
will declare their entrance into manhood.

MENTEITH

What is the tyrant Macbeth doing?

CAITHNESS

He is fortifying the great castle at Dunsinane.
Some say that he's gone mad; others, who hate him less,
call his actions courageous fury. But it's certainly clear

15   He cannot buckle his distempered cause
      Within the belt of rule.

ANGUS

                        Now does he feel
      His secret murders sticking on his hands;
      Now minutely revolts upbraid his faith-breach.
      Those he commands move only in command,
20   Nothing in love. Now does he feel his title
      Hang loose about him, like a giant's robe
      Upon a dwarfish thief.

MENTEITH

                        Who then shall blame
      His pestered senses to recoil and start,
      When all that is within him does condemn
      Itself for being there?

CAITHNESS

25   Well, march we on,
      To give obedience where 'tis truly owed.
      Meet we the med'cine of the sickly weal,
      And with him pour we, in our country's purge,
      Each drop of us.

LENNOX

                        Or so much as it needs
30   To dew the sovereign flower and drown the weeds.
      Make we our march towards Birnam.
                Exeunt, marching.

Scene iii: [*Dunsinane. In the castle.*] *Enter* MACBETH, *Doctor, and*
Attendants.

MACBETH

      Bring me no more reports. Let them fly all!
      Till Birnam Wood remove to Dunsinane
      I cannot taint with wear. What's the boy Malcolm?
      Was he not born of woman? The spirits that know
5   All mortal consequences have pronounced me thus:
      "Fear not, Macbeth; no man that's born of woman
      Shall e'er have power upon thee." Then fly, false thanes,
      And mingle with the English epicures.

15   that he can't manage to keep his sick and swollen cause
     within the bounds of self-control.

ANGUS
     Now he feels
     his hidden murders clinging to his hands.
     Now every minute there are new uprisings to protest his
        treachery.
     His followers act only because they are commanded to do so,
20   not out of love. Now he feels his title of King
     draped loosely around him, hanging like a giant's robe
     on a dwarf-like thief.

MENTEITH
     Then who can blame
     his tormented senses for being jumpy and easily startled,
     when his own conscience condemns
     what it finds in his inner thoughts?

CAITHNESS
25   Well, let's march on
     and pledge our obedience to a leader (i.e., Malcolm) who really
     deserves it. Let's meet the man who will cure our sick society
     and we'll pour with him—in this purgation of our country—
     each and every drop of our blood.

LENNOX
     Or as much blood as is needed
30   to water the flowers and drown the weeds.
     Let's march toward Birnam Wood.
        They exit, marching.

Act V, Scene iii: A room in the castle at Dunsinane. Enter MAC-
BETH, *accompanied by a Doctor and Attendants.*

MACBETH
     Don't bring me any more reports. Let all the thanes desert me!
     Until Birnam Wood comes here to Dunsinane,
     I can't be infected with fear. What is this boy Malcolm?
     Wasn't he born of woman? The spirits that foresee
5   the outcome of all human affairs have solemnly assured me:
     "Have no fear, Macbeth. No man born of woman
     shall ever overpower you." Then run away, traitorous thanes,
     and join the easy-living English.

The mind I sway by and the heart I bear
10   Shall never sag with doubt nor shake with fear.
        Enter Servant.
    The devil damn thee black, thou cream-faced loon!
    Where got'st thou that goose look?
SERVANT
    There is ten thousand——
MACBETH
                            Geese, villain?
SERVANT
                                    Soldiers, sir.
MACBETH
    Go prick thy face and over-red thy fear,
15   Thou lily-livered boy. What soldiers, patch?
    Death of thy soul! Those linen cheeks of thine
    Are counselors to fear. What soldiers, whey-face?
SERVANT
    The English force, so please you.
MACBETH
    Take thy face hence.
        [*Exit Servant.*]
                        Seyton!—I am sick at heart,
20   When I behold—Seyton, I say!—This push
    Will cheer me ever, or disseat me now.
    I have lived long enough. My way of life
    Is fall'n into the sear, the yellow leaf,
    And that which should accompany old age,
25   As honor, love, obedience, troops of friends,
    I must not look to have; but, in their stead,
    Curses not loud but deep, mouth-honor, breath,
    Which the poor heart would fain deny, and dare not.
    Seyton!
        Enter SEYTON.
SEYTON
    What's your gracious pleasure?
MACBETH
                            What news more?
30
SEYTON
    All is confirmed, my lord, which was reported.

The mind I am governed by and the heart I carry within me
shall never give in to doubt nor shake with fear.
>*Enter a Servant.*

May the devil turn you black, you white-faced lunatic!
Where did you get that stupid goose look?

SERVANT
There are ten thousand—

MACBETH
Geese, villain?

SERVANT
Soldiers, sir.

MACBETH
Go scratch your face and let the blood cover your fear with red,
you chicken-hearted boy. What soldiers, clown?
Damn your soul! Your white-linen cheeks
are advising others to be afraid too. What soldiers, cheese-face?

SERVANT
The English army, if you please.

MACBETH
Get your face out of here.
>*The Servant exits.*

Seyton! I am heartsick
when I see—Seyton, I'm calling you!—This attack
will make me happy forever or lose the throne for me right now.
I have lived long enough. My life-style
has been transformed into a shriveled and faded leaf,
and all those things which ought to go along with old age,
such as honor, love, obedience, crowds of friends,
I can't expect to have. Instead I get
curses, not voiced loudly but felt deeply, and respectful
    mouthings of courtesy, merely hot air,
which the timid speaker would like to deny but dares not.
Seyton!
>*Enter SEYTON.*

SEYTON
What is your royal pleasure?

MACBETH
Any further news?

SEYTON
All the reports have been confirmed, my lord.

MACBETH
I'll fight, till from my bones my flesh be hacked.
Give me my armor.

SEYTON
'Tis not needed yet.

MACBETH
I'll put it on.
35   Send out moe horses, skirr the country round.
Hang those that talk of fear. Give me mine armor.
How does your patient, doctor?

DOCTOR
Not so sick, my lord,
As she is troubled with thick-coming fancies
That keep her from her rest.

MACBETH
Cure her of that.
40   Canst thou not minister to a mind diseased,
Pluck from the memory a rooted sorrow,
Raze out the written troubles of the brain,
And with some sweet oblivious antidote
Cleanse the stuffed bosom of that perilous stuff
Which weighs upon the heart?

DOCTOR
Therein the patient
45   Must minister to himself.

MACBETH
Throw physic to the dogs, I'll none of it.
Come, put mine armor on. Give me my staff.
Seyton, send out.—Doctor, the thanes fly from me.—
50   Come, sir, dispatch. If thou couldst, doctor, cast
The water of my land, find her disease
And purge it to a sound and pristine health,
I would applaud thee to the very echo,
That should applaud again.—Pull 't off, I say.—
55   What rhubarb, senna, or what purgative drug,
Would scour these English hence? Hear'st thou of them?

MACBETH

I'll fight until my flesh is hacked from my bones.

Give me my armor.

SEYTON

You don't need it yet.

MACBETH

35   I'll put it on.

Send out more horsemen to search the countryside.

Hang those that talk of fear. Give me my armor.

How is your patient (i.e., Lady Macbeth), Doctor?

DOCTOR

She is not as sick physically, my lord,

as she is disturbed with an overwhelming mass of delusions

that interfere with her sleep.

MACBETH

40   That's what I want you to cure her of!

Can't you treat a disturbed mind;

uproot from the memory a deeply implanted sorrow,

erase all the troubles recorded in the brain,

and with some gentle, tranquilizing medicine

purify the over-full heart of that dangerous matter

which weighs it down?

DOCTOR

45   In such cases, the patient

must cure himself.

MACBETH

Then throw medicine to the dogs! I'll have nothing to do with it!

(*To Seyton*) Come, help me put on my armor. Give me my staff

of command.

Seyton, send out for more news. (*To Doctor*) Doctor, the thanes

are deserting me.

50   (*To Seyton*) All right, sir, hurry up. (*To Doctor*) Doctor, if you

could do

a urinanalysis of Scotland, diagnose her disease,

and cleanse my country to its former good health,

I would applaud you so loudly that the very echo

would sound as if you were being applauded again. (*To Seyton*)

Pull it off, I say.

55   (*To Doctor*) What rhubarb, senna, or other laxative plant

would rid us of these English forces? Have you heard of any

such medicines?

DOCTOR
    Ay, my good lord; your royal preparation
    Makes us hear something.
MACBETH
                                Bring it after me.
    I will not be afraid of death and bane
60 Till Birnam Forest come to Dunsinane.
        [*Exeunt* MACBETH *and* SEYTON.]

DOCTOR [*Aside*]
    Were I from Dunsinane away and clear,
    Profit again should hardly draw me here.
        Exit.

Scene iv: [*Country near Birnam Wood.*] *Drum and colors. Enter*
MALCOLM, SIWARD, MACDUFF, *Siward's Son*, MENTEITH, CAITH-
NESS, ANGUS, *and Soldiers, marching.*

MALCOLM
    Cousins, I hope the days are near at hand
    That chambers will be safe.
MENTEITH
                                We doubt it nothing.
SIWARD
    What wood is this before us?
MENTEITH
                                The Wood of Birnam.
MALCOLM
    Let every soldier hew him down a bough
5   And bear 't before him. Thereby shall we shadow
    The numbers of our host, and make discovery
    Err in report of us.
SOLDIERS
                    It shall be done.
SIWARD
    We learn no other but the confident tyrant
    Keeps still in Dunsinane, and will endure
    Our setting down before 't.

DOCTOR
  Yes, my good lord, your preparation for war
  sounds to me like such a remedy.

MACBETH (*to Seyton*)
  Bring the rest of the armor after me.
  I will have no fear of death and ruin
60 until Birnam Wood march to Dunsinane.
    MACBETH *and* SEYTON *exit.*

DOCTOR
  If I could get safely away from Dunsinane,
  it's unlikely that any fee would lure me back.
    He exits.

*Act V, Scene iv: The open country near Birnam Wood. Drums
and flags. Enter* MALCOLM, SIWARD, SIWARD'S SON, MAC-
DUFF, MENTEITH, CAITHNESS, ANGUS, *and Soldiers,
marching.*

MALCOLM
  Kinsmen, I hope the time is near
  when a man will be safe in his own home.

MENTEITH
  We have no doubt about it.

SIWARD
  What woods are these in front of us?

MENTEITH
  It's Birnam Wood.

MALCOLM
  I want every soldier to cut a branch down
5 and carry it in front of him. In this way we'll conceal
  the size of our force and trick the enemy reconnaisance
  into making a false report of us.

SOLDIERS
  We'll do it.

SIWARD
  We've discovered nothing except that the confident tyrant
  still remains in his castle at Dunsinane, and is prepared for
  our setting up a siege in front of it.

MALCOLM

10
　　　　　　　　　　　'Tis his main hope,
For where there is advantage to be gone
Both more and less have given him the revolt,
And none serve with him but constrainèd things
Whose hearts are absent too.

MACDUFF

　　　　　　　　　　Let our just censures
15
Attend the true event, and put we on
Industrious soldiership.

SIWARD

　　　　　　　　　The time approaches,
That will with due decision make us know
What we shall say we have and what we owe.
Thoughts speculative their unsure hopes relate,
20
But certain issue strokes must arbitrate:
Towards which advance the way.
　　　Exeunt, marching.

Scene v: [Dunsinane. Within the castle.] Enter MACBETH, SEYTON, *and Soldiers, with drum and colors.*

MACBETH

Hang out our banners on the outward walls.
The cry is still "They come!" Our castle's strength
Will laugh a siege to scorn. Here let them lie
Till famine and the ague eat them up.
5
Were they not forced with those that should be ours,
We might have met them dareful, beard to beard,
And beat them backward home.
　　　A cry within of women.
　　　　　　　　　　What is that noise?

SEYTON

It is the cry of women, my good lord.
　　　[Exit.]

MALCOLM
10   It's his chief hope.
      Whenever there is an opportunity to depart,
        both the great and the lowly have revolted against him
          (and fled).
      No one serves him but those who are forced to,
      and they don't have their hearts in it.

MACDUFF
      Let our true opinions
15   wait for the actual outcome of the battle, and let's apply
        ourselves
      with all our skill to being soldiers.

SIWARD
      The time is coming
      when we'll know the outcome exactly :
      what we claim to have, and what we really own.
      Speculation only gives us uncertain hopes ;
20   the real issues must be decided in battle.
      To hasten this decision, let the army advance.
          They exit, marching.

*Act V, Scene v: Within the outer fortifications of Macbeth's castle
at Dunsinane. Enter* MACBETH *and* SEYTON, *accompanied by
Soldiers. Drums and flags.*

MACBETH
      Fly our banners on the outer walls.
      I still hear the cry "They come!" Our castle's strength
      will make their siege a laughing matter. Let them stay here
      until famine and fever eat them up.
5   If they weren't reinforced with our deserters,
      we might have fought them boldly, man to man,
      and beat them back to their homes.
          A cry of women is heard from within the castle.
      What is that noise?

SEYTON
      It is women screaming, my good lord.
          He exits.

MACBETH

I have almost forgot the taste of fears:

10   The time has been, my senses would have cooled
To hear a night-shriek, and my fell of hair
Would at a dismal treatise rouse and stir
As life were in 't. I have supped full with horrors.
Direness, familiar to my slaughterous thoughts,
Cannot once start me.

[*Enter* SEYTON.]

15   Wherefore was that cry?

SEYTON

The Queen, my lord, is dead.

MACBETH

She should have died hereafter;
There would have been a time for such a word.*
Tomorrow, and tomorrow, and tomorrow

20   Creeps in this petty pace from day to day,
To the last syllable of recorded time;
And all our yesterdays have lighted fools
The way to dusty death. Out, out, brief candle!
Life's but a walking shadow, a poor player

25   That struts and frets his hour upon the stage
And then is heard no more. It is a tale
Told by an idiot, full of sound and fury
Signifying nothing.

Enter a Messenger.

Thou com'st to use thy tongue; thy story quickly!

MESSENGER

30   Gracious my lord,
I should report that which I say I saw,
But know not how to do 't.

MACBETH

                        Well, say, sir.

MESSENGER

As I did stand my watch upon the hill,
I looked toward Birnam, and anon, methought,
The wood began to move.

17-18 *She ... word* Editors have disputed the meaning of this passage.
Some see it as meaning: "She would have died sometime," while others read
it as: "Her death ought to have been put off to a more convenient time."

MACBETH

I have almost forgotten what fear tastes like.
Once I would have shivered
if I heard a shriek in the night; and if I read
a frightening story, my hair would stand on end
as if it were alive. I've had my fill of horrors.
Terror, which goes hand in hand with my bloody thoughts,
can no longer startle me.
  Enter SEYTON.
What was the cause of that cry?

SEYTON

My lord, the queen is dead.

MACBETH

She should have died later,
when I would have had the time to grieve at such news.
Tomorrow follows tomorrow and is followed by tomorrow,
feebly creeping from day to day
to the last syllable of written history,
and our entire past has lighted the way for fools
down the path to dusty death. Burn out, burn out, you short
  candle of life.
A man's life is only a walking shadow, a poor actor
who swaggers and paces about the stage for an hour
and then is never heard from again. Life is a tale
told by an idiot, full of noise and rage,
but meaning nothing.
  Enter a Messenger.
You've come to tell me something; out with it quickly.

MESSENGER

My gracious lord,
I wish to report what I swear I saw,
but I don't know how to do it.

MACBETH

Well, out with it, man.

MESSENGER

While I was on guard duty on the hill,
I looked toward Birnam Wood, and soon I thought I saw
the forest begin to move.

MACBETH

35   Liar and slave!

MESSENGER

Let me endure your wrath, if 't be not so.
Within this three mile may you see it coming;
I say a moving grove.

MACBETH

If thou speak'st false,
Upon the next tree shalt thou hang alive,
40   Till famine cling thee. If thy speech be sooth,
I care not if thou dost for me as much.
I pull in resolution, and begin
To doubt th' equivocation of the fiend
That lies like truth: "Fear not, till Birnam Wood
45   Do come to Dunsinane!" And now a wood
Comes toward Dunsinane. Arm, arm, and out!
If this which he avouches does appear,
There is nor flying hence nor tarrying here.
I 'gin to be aweary of the sun,
50   And wish th' estate o' th' world were now undone.
Ring the alarum bell! Blow wind, come wrack!
At least we'll die with harness on our back.
        Exeunt.

Scene vi: [*Dunsinane. Before the castle.*] *Drum and colors. Enter*
MALCOLM, SIWARD, MACDUFF, *and their army, with boughs.*

MALCOLM

Now near enough. Your leavy screens throw down,
And show like those you are. You, worthy uncle,
Shall, with my cousin, your right noble son,
Lead our first battle. Worthy Macduff and we
5   Shall take upon 's what else remains to do,
According to our order.

SIWARD

Fare you well.
Do we but find the tyrant's power tonight,
Let us be beaten, if we cannot fight.

MACBETH

35   Liar and slave!

MESSENGER

If I'm lying, I'll take whatever punishment your anger may give.
You can see it coming less than three miles off.
I say again: a moving wood.

MACBETH

If you're lying,
you'll hang alive from the nearest tree,
40   until you shrivel up from hunger. But if you're speaking the truth,
I don't care if you do the same for me.
I'm losing my confidence and begin
to suspect the double meanings of that devil
who can make lies sound like truth: "Fear not, till Birnam Wood
45   comes to Dunsinane!" And now a wood
actually is coming toward Dunsinane. To arms, to arms, and attack!
If what he reports really does appear,
we can neither flee nor remain.
I'm beginning to grow weary of life
50   and wish the orderly structure of the world was destroyed.
Ring the battle bell! Let the wind blow; let ruin come!
At least we'll die with armor on our backs.
       They exit.

Act V, Scene vi: In front of Macbeth's castle at Dunsinane. Enter
MALCOLM, SIWARD, MACDUFF, *and Soldiers, carrying branches. Drums and flags.*

MALCOLM

We're close enough now. Throw away the concealing branches
and reveal yourselves. You, my worthy uncle Siward,
and your most noble son, my kinsman,
lead the first battalion. Worthy Macduff and I
5   will carry out whatever else remains to be done
according to the battle plan.

SIWARD

Farewell.
If we face the tyrant's army tonight
and can't fight, we deserve to be beaten.

MACDUFF
Make all our trumpets speak; give them all breath,

10   Those clamorous harbingers of blood and death.
Exeunt, Alarums continued.

Scene vii: [Another part of the field.] Enter MACBETH.

MACBETH
They have tied me to a stake; I cannot fly,
But bearlike I must fight the course.* What's he
That was not born of woman? Such a one
Am I to fear, or none.
Enter YOUNG SIWARD.
YOUNG SIWARD
What is thy name?
MACBETH
                    Thou'lt be afraid to hear it.

5

YOUNG SIWARD
No; though thou call'st thyself a hotter name
Than any is in hell.
MACBETH
                    My name's Macbeth.
YOUNG SIWARD
The devil himself could not pronounce a title
More hateful to mine ear.
MACBETH
                    No, nor more fearful.
YOUNG SIWARD

10   Thou liest, abhorrèd tyrant; with my sword
I'll prove the lie thou speak'st.
Fight, and YOUNG SIWARD *slain.*
MACBETH
                    Thou wast born of woman.
But swords I smile at, weapons laugh to scorn,
Brandished by man that's of a woman born.
Exit.
Alarums. Enter MACDUFF.

---

2 *bearlike ... course* A popular sport of Shakespeare's time was bear-
baiting, in which a bear was chained to a stake in a ring or arena and

MACDUFF
Sound all our trumpets, give them a full blast,
those loud announcers of blood and death.
They exit, while the trumpets sound the call to arms.

*Act V, Scene vii: A battlefield near Macbeth's castle at Dunsinane.
Enter MACBETH.*

MACBETH
They have tied me to a post. I can't escape,
but like a tethered bear I must fight this round to the end.
   Who is it
that was not born of woman? He is
the one I have to fear—nobody else.
   Enter YOUNG SIWARD.

YOUNG SIWARD
What's your name?

MACBETH
You'd be frightened if you heard it.

YOUNG SIWARD
No, not even if you've got a name hotter
than any in hell.

MACBETH
My name's Macbeth.

YOUNG SIWARD
The devil himself could not speak a name
more hateful to my ear.

MACBETH
No, nor more frightening to you.

YOUNG SIWARD
You are a liar, despised tyrant. With my sword
I'll prove that it's a lie you speak.
   They fight, and Young Siward is killed.

MACBETH
You were a man born of woman.
I smile at swords, laugh scornfully at weapons
wielded by a man that is born of woman.
   He exits. Calls to arms continue. Enter MACDUFF.

---

ferocious dogs were released to attack him. "Course" was a common term
for "bout."

168   *Macbeth*

MACDUFF
    That way the noise is. Tyrant, show thy face!
15   If thou be'st slain and with no stroke of mine,
    My wife and children's ghosts will haunt me still.
    I cannot strike at wretched kerns, whose arms
    Are hired to bear their staves. Either thou, Macbeth,
    Or else my sword, with an unbattered edge,
20   I sheathe again undeeded. There thou shouldst be;
    By this great clatter, one of greatest note
    Seems bruited. Let me find him, Fortune!
    And more I beg not.
        Exit. Alarums.
        Enter MALCOLM *and* SIWARD.
SIWARD
    This way, my lord. The castle's gently rend'red:
25   The tyrant's people on both sides do fight;
    The noble thanes do bravely in the war;
    The day almost itself professes yours,
    And little is to do.
MALCOLM
                We have met with foes
    That strike beside us.
SIWARD
                Enter, sir, the castle.
        Exeunt. Alarum.

Scene viii: [Another part of the field.] Enter MACBETH.

MACBETH
    Why should I play the Roman fool,* and die
    On mine own sword? Whiles I see lives the gashes
    Do better upon them.
        Enter MACDUFF.
MACDUFF
                Turn, hell-hound, turn!
MACBETH
    Of all men else I have avoided thee.
5   But get thee back! My soul is too much charged
    With blood of thine already.

---

    1 *Roman fool* ·Roman gentlemen traditionally committed suicide to
avoid dishonor in defeat. Thus we see Brutus and Cassius commit suicide in
Shakespeare's *Julius Caesar* and Antony do so in *Antony and Cleopatra.*

MACDUFF

The battle noises are coming from over there. Tyrant, show
your face!
15   If you've already been killed without a blow from me,
the ghosts of my wife and children will go on haunting me.
I can't fight with poor infantrymen who
are paid to carry spears. Either I fight with you, Macbeth,
or I will put this sword, with its unhacked edge,
20   into its sheath again unused. Macbeth, you should be where the
battle is fiercest;
from the great clatter over there, someone of highest rank
seems to be announced. Good Fortune, let me find him!
I ask for nothing else.
     He exits. Calls to arms. Enter MALCOLM *and* SIWARD.

SIWARD

This way, my lord. The castle surrendered without a struggle.
25   The tyrant's people are fighting on our side as well as his.
Your noble thanes are fighting valiantly.
This day of battle almost declares itself a victory for you,
and there is little more to accomplish.

MALCOLM

I've fought with foes
who deliberately avoided hitting me.

SIWARD

Come, enter the castle, sir.
     They exit. A call to arms.

Act V, Scene viii: Another part of the battlefield in front of Macbeth's castle. Enter MACBETH.

MACBETH

Why should I act like a Roman fool and commit suicide
with my own sword? While there are still living enemies around,
the wounds look better on them.
     Enter MACDUFF.

MACDUFF

Turn around, hell-hound, turn!

MACBETH

Of all other men, you are the one I have purposely avoided.
5   Get back! My soul is already weighted down
with your family's blood.

MACDUFF

                      I have no words:
My voice is in my sword, thou bloodier villain
Than terms can give thee out!
    Fight. Alarum.

MACBETH

                     Thou losest labor:
As easy mayst thou the intrenchant air

10   With thy keen sword impress as make me bleed.
Let fall thy blade on vulnerable crests;
I bear a charmèd life, which must not yield
To one of woman born.

MACDUFF

                  Despair thy charm,
And let the angel whom thou still hast served

15   Tell thee, Macduff was from his mother's womb
Untimely ripped.*

MACBETH

Accursèd be that tongue that tells me so,
For it hath cowed my better part of man!
And be these juggling fiends no more believed,

20   That palter with us in a double sense;
That keep the word of promise to our ear,
And break it to our hope. I'll not fight with thee.

MACDUFF

Then yield thee, coward,
And live to be the show and gaze o' th' time:

25   We'll have thee, as our rarer monsters are,
Painted upon a pole, and underwrit,
"Here may you see the tyrant."

MACBETH

                   I will not yield,
To kiss the ground before young Malcolm's feet,
And to be baited with the rabble's curse.

30   Though Birnam Wood be come to Dunsinane,
And thou opposed, being of no woman born,
Yet I will try the last. Before my body
I throw my warlike shield. Lay on, Macduff;

---

16 *Untimely ripped* i.e., Caesarean section, the operation of taking a
child from the uterus by cutting through the walls of the abdomen.

MACDUFF
I'll not exchange words with you;
I'll talk only with my sword, you villain, more murderous
than words can describe!
They fight. A call to arms.

MACBETH
You're wasting your energy.
You can as easily cut the impenetrable air
with your sharp sword as wound me.
Use your sword against armor that is vulnerable.
I live a charmed life that cannot be taken
by anyone born of woman.

MACDUFF
Give up hope for your charm, then,
and let the corrupted angel you still serve
inform you that Macduff was from his mother's womb
prematurely delivered.

MACBETH
Let the tongue that tells me this be cursed,
because it has drained me of my manliness!
And let those deceiving witches never again be believed,
who trick us with their double meanings:
that fulfill the promising words we hear,
but fail us in what we expect. I don't want to fight with you.

MACDUFF
Then surrender, coward,
and become the show and public spectacle of our age.
We'll advertise you as we do our choicest freaks,
by a painting hung on a pole, and we'll write under it,
"Here you can see the tyrant."

MACBETH
I will not surrender
to kiss the ground before young Malcolm's feet
and to be taunted by the mob's curses.
Though Birnam Wood has come to Dunsinane,
and you who I fight are not born of woman,
yet I will fight to the end. In front of my body
I raise my battle-shield. Strike hard, Macduff, and

And damned be him that first cries "Hold, enough!"

Exeunt, fighting. Alarums.

[Re-]enter fighting, and MACBETH *slain. [Exit* MACDUFF, *with* MACBETH.] *Retreat and flourish. Enter, with drum and colors,* MALCOLM, SIWARD, ROSS, *Thanes, and Soldiers.*

MALCOLM

35   I would the friends we miss were safe arrived.

SIWARD

Some must go off; and yet, by these I see,
So great a day as this is cheaply bought.

MALCOLM

Macduff is missing, and your noble son.

ROSS

Your son, my lord, has paid a soldier's debt:
40   He only lived but till he was a man;
The which no sooner had his prowess confirmed
In the unshrinking station where he fought,
But like a man he died.

SIWARD

                         Then he is dead?

ROSS

Ay, and brought off the field. Your cause of sorrow
45   Must not be measured by his worth, for then
It hath no end.

SIWARD

                         Had he his hurts before?

ROSS

Ay, on the front.

SIWARD

                         Why then, God's soldier be he!
Had I as many sons as I have hairs,
I would not wish them to a fairer death:
And so his knell is knolled.

MALCOLM

                         He's worth more sorrow,
50   And that I'll spend for him.

cursed be the one who first cries, "Stop, I've had enough!"
> *They exit, fighting. Calls to arms. Then they re-enter still*
> *fighting. Macbeth is killed.* MACDUFF *exits with the*
> *body of Macbeth. A retreat is sounded and a flourish of*
> *trumpets. Enter* MALCOLM, SIWARD, ROSS, *Thanes,*
> *and Soldiers, with drum and flags.*

MALCOLM
35 I wish that our missing friends were here, safe and sound.

SIWARD
Some must die in battle, and yet, as I look at those around me,
I see that this great day of victory was gained without much
loss of life.

MALCOLM
Macduff and your noble son are still missing.

ROSS
My lord, your son has paid a soldier's debt with his own life.
40 He only lived long enough to become a man.
No sooner had he proved his manhood by the bravery
with which he fought and held his position,
than he died like the man he was.

SIWARD
Then he is dead?

ROSS
Yes, and carried off the field. Your reason for sorrow
45 must not be in proportion to the worth of your son, for then
it would have no end.

SIWARD
Were his wounds in front of his body?

ROSS
Yes, in front.

SIWARD
Why then he's a soldier with God in heaven!
If I had as many sons as I have hairs,
I couldn't wish a better death for any of them.
So, then, his death knell has been rung.

MALCOLM
50 He deserves more show of sorrow than that,
and I'll give him all due formalities.

SIWARD
                              He's worth no more.
They say he parted well and paid his score:
And so God be with him! Here comes newer comfort.
        Enter MACDUFF, *with* MACBETH'*s head.*
MACDUFF
Hail, King! for so thou art: behold, where stands
55   Th' usurper's cursèd head. The time is free.
I see thee compassed with thy kingdom's pearl,
That speak my salutation in their minds,
Whose voices I desire aloud with mine:
Hail, King of Scotland!
ALL
                              Hail, King of Scotland!
        Flourish.
MALCOLM
60   We shall not spend a large expense of time
Before we reckon with your several loves,
And make us even with you. My thanes and kinsmen,
Henceforth be earls, the first that ever Scotland
In such an honor named. What's more to do,
65   Which would be planted newly with the time—
As calling home our exiled friends abroad
That fled the snares of watchful tyranny,
Producing forth the cruel ministers
Of this dead butcher and his fiendlike queen,
70   Who, as 'tis thought, by self and violent hands
Took off her life—this, and what needful else
That calls upon us, by the grace of Grace
We will perform in measure, time, and place:
So thanks to all at once and to each one,
75   Whom we invite to see us crowned at Scone.
        Flourish. Exeunt Omnes.
                      F I N I S

SIWARD

He deserves nothing more.

They say he died well and did his duty,

and so may God be with him! Here comes a more recent comfort
Enter MACDUFF, *carrying Macbeth's head on a pole.*

MACDUFF

Hail, King! for so you are. Behold where I've stuck

55 the usurper's damnable head. The world is liberated.

I see that you are surrounded by the pearls of your kingdom
(i. e., your thanes),

who are thinking the very greeting I now make.

I want their voices to join aloud with mine.

Hail, King of Scotland!

ALL

Hail, King of Scotland!
Flourish played by trumpets.

MALCOLM

60 I will not let much time go by

before I reward the loyalty of each of you

and repay you for what you've done. My thanes and kinsmen

will henceforth be called earls—the first that Scotland

has raised to such an honorable title. Whatever else should
be done,

65 whatever else ought to be started anew in this period—

such as calling home our exiled friends from abroad

who left to escape the traps of spying tyranny,

bringing forward and exposing the ruthless agents

of this dead butcher and his devilish queen

70 who, it is thought, with her own violent hands,

took her life—these matters and whatever else seems necessary

and requires my attention, by the grace of God,

will be done properly and at the right time and place.

I give thanks to all, and to each and every one,

whom I invite to see me crowned at Scone.
A flourish of trumpets. They exit.

THE PLAY IN REVIEW:
A Teacher and Student Supplement

Between Acts: Study Questions

Act I

1. **What mood is established at the beginning of the play?**

By opening with the witches, Shakespeare creates an eerie mood, an atmosphere permeated with evil. A reversal of usual values is apparent in the witches' chant, "Fair is foul and foul is fair" — the keynote of the drama. Although human initiative brings forth the evil which dominates the play, the witches personify that evil and give it substance.

Their use of animals as "familiars" to do their bidding foreshadows Macbeth's eventual role; he too will commit animal acts suggested by the witches. The animals symbolize the world Shakespeare creates in *Macbeth*: a primitive culture, a dog-eat-dog fight for supremacy, without the veneer of civilization.

2. **How does Scene 2 introduce the absent Macbeth?**

Although past behavior and many compliments create a favorable portrait of Macbeth, there is a hint of his real nature in Duncan's first line, "What bloody man is that?" The words refer to a wounded soldier, but they also foreshadow Macbeth's later character and the importance of blood throughout the play. Macbeth dominates this scene though he does not appear in it. His physical courage is praised at great length, but his moral timbre is at this point unknown.

Macbeth, as the king's loyal subject, has defeated a rebellion led by Macdonwald, and his strength and valor have won the admiration of all. The honor Macbeth receives here is in sharp contrast to the horror and scorn his subsequent actions will produce.

Finally, Duncan ends the scene by declaring that a traitor, the thane of Cawdor, is to be executed and his title bestowed upon Macbeth. This action creates a dramatic irony: Cawdor's treason, as well as his title, is passed to his heir. As Duncan innocently remarks, "What he hath lost noble Macbeth hath won."

3. Were the witches intended to be real?

Perhaps. Superstition played an important part in Renaissance thinking, and the supernatural element gives this drama additional zest and excitement. The witches create suspense, irony, and horror.

Shakespeare gives no explicit stage directions about the appearance of the witches. From the way Banquo and Macbeth start in surprise on encountering them, we infer that their appearance is startling. Yet the two soldiers react merely in surprise, not in horror. The witches then are not monsters. Banquo judges them women by their shape, then notes their strange clothing, their withered look, and their beards.

4. How do Banquo and Macbeth react to the witches?

Macbeth's first words "So foul and fair a day," echoing the witches' "Fair is foul and foul is fair," link him immediately to the powers of evil. His remark also reflects his moral problem; when good and evil are combined, it is sometimes hard to distinguish one from the other. Thus a prophecy of good fortune may carry with it undertones of doom.

Banquo starts at seeing the witches. He notes that they look unearthly and thus seem almost hallucinatory. This emphasizes the ambiguity of evil: they seem wicked, as their prophecies seem true, yet the real wickedness must be initiated by Macbeth.

The witches have opened the scene with wicked intent executed in terms of petty mischief. Only when they speak with Macbeth does the possibility of true evil arise, and their real power take shape in a human instrument, Macbeth.

177

5. **How do Macbeth and Banquo receive the news from Ross and Angus?**

Again, this is both fair and foul. It is good news but Macbeth fears it, for is it not a token that the witches' prophecy may come true entirely? They have promised him Cawdor and he has been given Cawdor; perhaps their prophecy of the crown may also be fulfilled. If so, he fears that he will not be merely a bystander, that he must grasp it for himself. But this is a dreadful thought; he thrusts it from him, reasoning that if destiny would have him king, destiny can accomplish it without his own action. At this point he is content to wait and let fate take its course.

Banquo notes that Macbeth is bemused by his new title and wonders if there will be consequences. He is impartial enough, however, to fear that the announcement may have been included in the prophecy, he does not change his attitude toward the crown. His is a conscious decision, a deliberate refusal to heed the witches' promise of power.

6. **What images do Duncan's words in Scene 4 conjure up?**

He speaks first on Cawdor's execution, of Cawdor's poise in facing death. These words will also apply to Macbeth at the end of the drama. Then he turns to Macbeth with unfeigned affection. At this point in the drama, the name Macbeth is almost always preceded by some descriptive term bestowing honor. "Noble Macbeth," "worthy Macbeth," "brave Macbeth" — these are stark contrast to the play's conclusion when his is a name to frighten children.

Duncan speaks at length of what he owes Macbeth, more than he can repay. Unfortunately, the one honor that might satisfy Macbeth is whisked away when Duncan names his son Malcolm heir to the throne. Now Macbeth can only gain the crown through bloodshed.

Giving Macbeth a motive for murder, Duncan seals his doom by facilitating the means and opportunity. He proposes to visit Inverness, Macbeth's castle, as guest of his friend, kinsman, and subject.

7. How is Lady Macbeth characterized in Scene 5?

Learning of the witches' prophecy, she is roused to action and plans for the immediate future. Apparently she is both more ambitious and more action-oriented than the sensitive and contemplative Macbeth. She speaks of murder as if it were a trifle, a single effort in a larger program, and summons up all her ferocity and will to aid her purpose. Even so, the very force of her words tells against her. A famous Shakespearean line from another play comes to mind: "Methinks she doth protest too much." Surely, if Lady Macbeth were the monster she proclaims herself to be, she would not have to urge herself on in terms of such ruthlessness, rejecting even her femininity.

8. What is the relationship between Macbeth and his wife?

Theirs is a genuine love. Even in contemplating murder and kingship, he addresses her as the "dearest partner of my greatness" and later speaks to her as "my dearest love" and "dearest chuck." The murder is a gauge of their closeness; she wants what she thinks is due him, he is carrying out her apparent desires.

9. What is Lady Macbeth's evaluation of her husband?

At this point she is the dominant personality and knows it. Even though she loves her husband dearly, she is able to make a clear-eyed evaluation of him; he wants the crown, he has ambition, but he wants the title without effort. He will not stir forth to grasp it, certainly not to do murder. For her, the very act of wanting renders doing superfluous; if he wants to be king, it follows without saying that he must do anything to achieve that ambition. She is herself willing to commit any act to help him attain his apparent destiny.

10. What is the effect of Duncan's words in Scene 6?

His compliments on the castle which is to be the scene of his death, and his affectionate regard for Macbeth, are colored by the reader's uneasy knowledge of what is ahead. Lady Macbeth does not play the hypocrite too obviously; though Duncan speaks often of the "love" they show him, she responds in terms of "service." Finally, his cheerful reference to a songbird carries hidden horror: Lady Macbeth has just invoked the raven, feathered omen of doom.

11. What is the attitude of Macbeth's soliloquy in Scene 7?

Contemplating an irrevocable deed, Macbeth faces the action not with anticipation of reward, but with full acknowledgment of the horror he plans. He admits he has no real motive but uncontrolled ambition; Duncan is apparently an able monarch and has treated Macbeth well. The visit to Inverness places Macbeth in a position of double trust — he is both Duncan's subject and his host. The law of hospitality is an unwritten one, and breaking it defies customs more ancient than king and nation.

Just as he knows himself well enough to admit that pure ambition is his motive (neither he nor Lady Macbeth ever deceive themselves or each other with noble reasons for the murder), he is honest about his fears. He does not consider eternal damnation; the metaphysical is outside the scope of this hardy soldier. He considers instead earthly punishment. He would endure Hell if he could safely accomplish his crime in this life.

12. What is Lady Macbeth's function in Scene 7?

She brings Macbeth back from musing to the need for action. She details the plan they have made, a careful, emotionless outline which they have evidently discussed at some prior time. While she prepares her household to entertain Duncan, she prepares her husband for murder.

13. **Why is the topic of Lady Macbeth's womanliness raised again?**

Again she denies her femininity, blunting Macbeth's conscience with words of violence and action. She speaks particularly of her strong will; her mind set on a course, she would even dash out the brains of her own child. In parting, Macbeth tells her to "bring forth men children only" as a compliment to her courage. These two comments raise the question, not a central one, of whether Macbeth and his wife are childless. She says here that she has had children, yet later in the play (Act IV, Scene 3) Macduff says of Macbeth, "He has no children." Is this why thought of Banquo's descendants on the throne so rankles Macbeth?

Perhaps this enigma also serves to emphasize the isolation of Macbeth and his wife. The other main characters are linked to humanity through their posterity: Duncan and his sons, Macduff and his pathetic family, Banquo and Fleance. Macbeth and Lady Macbeth are apparently without family association. For the purpose of this drama, they epitomize destructiveness, and by the act of murder they cut themselves off from the creativeness of procreation. Thus, in a dramatic sense, they are incapable of having children.

Act II

14. **What is the significance of Banquo's talk with Fleance in Scene 1?**

This is a quiet moment, an interlude of peace. Yet the scene is not without dramatic import, for it is midnight, the witching hour. This conversation functions as the lull before the storm, a contrast to the horrors which follow.

Fleance's presence here impresses the reader with the fact that Banquo has an heir. In terms of plot, Fleance indirectly spells ruin for Macbeth; thematically, his existence stresses the continuation of Banquo's life-force.

Banquo mentions that he has been unable to sleep, a reminder that the witches' prophecies were disturbing to him as well as to Macbeth. Banquo, however, has refused to allow himself to consider the alluring predictions. It is as if the prophecies were an infection to which Macbeth succumbed while Banquo, through resolution and will power, consciously refused to let them enflame him.

15. **What is the significance of the dagger in Scene 1?**

This is the first of many apparitions which will confront Macbeth. He is a man of sensitivity and imagination, visualizing with full horror the scene which lies ahead. Interestingly enough, it is the dagger he sees, not the throne — the appalling means, rather than the attractive end. His confrontation with the dagger makes the murder real and vivid. Since the killing occurs offstage, its horror must be embodied by suspense and tension before and after the act itself.

16. **Describe Lady Macbeth's composure in Scene 2.**

Though she maintains control, she must take a drink as stimulus. This is the first sign that she may not have her emotions as tautly leashed as she boasts. Her mention that the sleeping Duncan resembles her own father is another human touch which prepares for her intense inability to cope with guilt and stress later in the play. The tension of the moment builds with whispered speeches and the harrowing noises which attend the murder.

17. **What is the effect of Macbeth's entrance after the murder?**

Macbeth returns literally dripping with blood, so that the killing becomes undeniably real. Gore brings home the actuality of the deed; the nightmare is not over, it has only begun. Macbeth babbles on about the killing, the words of the grooms, his frightening inability to pray. Each of these ideas has definite thematic consequence, but their major impact is to intensify the gruesomeness of driving a knife into a living human being. The deed is appalling, every bit as awful as Macbeth had feared it would be.

18. **What is the irony of Lady Macbeth's comfort?**

Again she takes the lead, soothing him, urging him to ignore these little omens. Yet actually it will be *her* sleep which is interrupted by nightmares, *her* bloodstains which will prove ineradicable.

19. **What is the function of the porter in Scene 3?**

The entrance of the porter has two important functions. First, and most important, the knocking on the gate thematically sounds out the total isolation to which Macbeth and his lady have condemned themselves. With their inhuman act, they have drawn a boundary between themselves and the rest of humanity, created a separate hell of fearsome noises, bloodstains, and alliance with darkness. The porter says, in fact, that he is knocking on the gate of hell. But Macbeth's crime does not bring with it an indictment of all mankind; a better world exists, and the porter's entrance is meant to typify the world of decency. During the murders of Duncan and his servants, ordinary time stands still; the outside world is eliminated. Then Shakespeare brings us back swiftly from the horror of slaughter to the normal, everyday world which will not allow such horror to go unpunished. The knocking at the gate

signifies that the pulses of life are beginning to beat
again. There is a greater meaning to life, a design
which does not permit murder, and with the knocking
that design is once more in operation.

Secondly, after the grim tension of the preceding
scenes, the babbling of the porter provides a kind of
comic relief. His remarks are shrewd and down to earth
and function as an outlet, a release for the grim tension
they follow. Note that his speech is in prose, running
on and on, as opposed to the measured iambic pen-
tameter in which most of the dialogue is phrased.

20. How is attention focused on Macduff?

It is important that Macduff, later to be Macbeth's
nemesis, be brought into central focus now, and this is
done in two ways. First, it is he who converses with the
porter, so that the dramatic spotlight which accom-
panies the porter's entrance includes him. Secondly,
when the grim news of Duncan's death is pronounced,
Macbeth not only names the grooms as killers but
states that he has taken their lives. It is Macduff who,
with utter candor and no semantic evasion, asks
directly, "Wherefore did you so?"

21. Why does Lady Macbeth faint?

This action may be a sign of human weakness on Lady
Macbeth's part, presaging her later inability to cope
with stress. On the other hand, perhaps it is a tactical
maneuver. Macbeth has shown signs of weakening (his
description of the murdered Duncan is wildly emotional) and now Macduff questions him bluntly. It may
be that she feigns a swoon to divert attention from her
husband.

22. Why are there unnatural omens during the night?

In Renaissance philosophy, the cosmos is a pattern of
interwoven planes. In order to achieve universal har-

mony, each element must function correctly in its own sphere. If disorder erupts at one level, there will be chaos throughout the universe.

Since memories of civil strife intensified the Elizabethans' desire for order, they made political obedience paramount in the chain of being. If a single primacy were overthrown, all nature would react. Should a subject kill a king, a heinous crime, the jackal might attack the lion, weeds would overtake the roses, etc. There is no such thing as individual doom because interdependence joins fate at all levels of the chain. It is no wonder that all nature shows signs of outrage, as reported in this scene and in the subsequent conversation between the Old Man and Ross.

23. **Why does Macbeth comment that he wishes himself dead?**

This is the first hint that all may not be well once the murder is accomplished. The witches' prophecies and the urgings of his wife contained no hint that Macbeth would suffer guilt. All has apparently gone as planned: he was not discovered during the act; no one has directly contradicted his explanation of Duncan's death; and he expects to gain the throne. Yet he regrets to the depth of his being the murder of the old man. Even now, at the moment of success, he wishes he could undo his act. These few lines foreshadow his later despair.

24. **How do Duncan's sons react when they learn of the murder?**

Malcolm and Donalbain seem stunned, but they are still able to sense danger. They seem to know that peril surrounds them, that this is not the place to mourn or even to discuss their fears. Unable to accept Macbeth's explanation, they plan immediate flight.

25. **What is the effect of the old man's talk in Scene 4?**

Again, the words affirm belief in the chain of being; Macbeth's act has disrupted the entire cosmos. Strange and unnatural happenings occur as a result of this crime, a crime in which a subject killed a king, a man murdered his kinsman, a host slew a guest. This conversation also reflects the action from the closed circle of Macbeth's court outward to the nation as a whole, intensifying the scope of the crime.

26. **What is the significance of Macduff's comments?**

His failure to attend the coronation sets him apart from the general allegiance to the new king and queen, presaging his final alienation from them. However, he states no overt suspicion of the new monarch; though he speaks with an undertone of uneasiness, he presents the official version of Duncan's death.

Act III

27. **In Scene 1, how does Macbeth react to success?**

In this soliloquy, he realizes that to be king is meaningless unless he can relax his fears. This is the delusion which haunts him: he can never be "safely thus," for the danger lies within. By his act of treachery and murder, he has created a world of his own against which every man is a threat.

There is never any intimation that Macbeth is enjoying his new position; his attitude is one of tension, anxiety, and fear. It is difficult to remember that he is king. It seems that, with the killing of Duncan, he has established himself as a murderer, no more and no less, forever. His reign hinges on the need to carry out another murder, and yet another.

Note the foreshadowing in the exchange between Banquo and Macbeth. "Fail not our feast," says Macbeth, and Banquo responds, "My lord, I will not," a pledge his ghost is later to honor. Banquo obviously suspects him but has no plans to put his suspicions into action. Macbeth, however, has already taken steps to rid himself of the fear which Banquo personifies. His meticulous questioning of Banquo about the length of Banquo's ride is a hint that he has a special interest.

28. How does Macbeth arouse the murderers?

He enflames them with lies about Banquo, which is a new and base sort of treachery for him. These are hired assassins and Macbeth despises their kind; he says they only pass for men. Yet he has reached the point where he can use such dirty instruments as these.

29. In Scene 2, is Lady Macbeth enjoying her new position?

No, perhaps even less than Macbeth. After all, there was never any suggestion prior to the crime that she longed to be queen; what she wished was to see Macbeth as king. The knowledge that he is without enjoyment of the monarchy must sadden her and, as she notes, anticipation is destroyed by realization. Guilt eventually overwhelms her.

30. Why does Macbeth keep his attack on Banquo a secret from her?

In the previous murder, Lady Macbeth was both instigator and planner, alibi and accomplice to the actual deed. She dominated Macbeth's better nature and spurred him on to murder. Now Macbeth has moved beyond her, no longer in need of support or guidance. Evil has become so much a part of him that his cunning surpasses even her.

31. Why does Macbeth invoke the night?

The night is the power of darkness, to which he allied himself at the time of Duncan's murder and whose metaphysical aid he needs now. Evil is symbolically associated with darkness. The witches are "secret, black and midnight hags" and, on a literal level, wickedness seems more easily carried out under cover of night.

32. Who is the third assassin at Banquo's murder?

The third man's identity has been the subject of much debate, though it is not a crucial question in terms of plot. Some scholars have suggested that it may have been Macbeth himself, wanting to take a personal hand in this important deed. His later surprise and agony at Fleance's escape would then become a show to disguise his bitterness as well as his involvement.

The literal explanation given in the text — that Macbeth has merely sent a third man to help them — is revealing also. Conditions have degenerated to the point that Macbeth cannot trust even hired assassins to do their job; he must have additional spies on hand to see that the bloody work is done properly.

33. How does Banquo react to the attack?

He knows immediately what is happening. His distrust of Macbeth and suspicions about Duncan's murder have prepared him. Accepting the imminence of his own death, he thinks only of Fleance's escape. This touch of humanity sets him off from Macbeth, the destroyer; Banquo is both creator and protector of Fleance.

34. What is the importance of Fleance's escape?

This is the turning point in the drama. All of Macbeth's murders are now futile and, in unendurable agony, he knows this. In order to void the witches' prophecy that Banquo will found a dynasty of kings, he must annihilate Banquo's entire line. Fleance's escape destroys his own hope for the future.

Macbeth's agony foreshadows the irony of the witches' prophecy and reveals the chaos of his mind.

How can he hope to trust the witches without doubt as long as they are in his favor, yet try to circumvent them when they promise good to someone else?

35. How does Macbeth delude himself in Scene 4?

Ever since the prophecy, Macbeth has felt just one murder away from contentment. Beginning with Duncan, Macbeth has believed that if only he can silence one mouth, eliminate one threat, he will be at ease. This is delusion, of course, for he can never escape the guilty turmoil of his own mind. However, because of this delusion he has killed Banquo. Now, lacking Fleance, he fastens upon Macduff as the "one threat" to be eliminated.

36. What is the importance of Banquo's ghost?

Macbeth is a man of sensitivity and imagination; he visualized a dagger previous to Duncan's killing. Now he visualizes Banquo's ghost, revealing both his sense of guilt and the main source of sympathy for the protagonists of this drama. For Macbeth and his lady continue to suffer as much as those they have wronged, and he is as much caught in a trap as those he hunts. Worse, the scene ends with the ominous words, "We are but young in deed."

37. How does Lady Macbeth respond to Macbeth's outburst?

When Macbeth experiences what must seem a hallucination (for the apparition appears to no one but him), she intercedes to hide his guilt. As she had acted to prevent his exposure after Duncan's death, so she acts now to persuade the guests to ignore him. It is apparent that she is controlling herself despite tension, fear, and guilt.

38. What is revealed about conditions in Scotland?

The country has become a brutal police state where assassins are hired by those in power. Macbeth admits that he keeps paid informers to spy upon his subjects. Macduff is now the object of his fears and the intended victim of the next purge.

39. **What is the purpose of Hecate's interview with the witches?**

This scene foreshadows Macbeth's confrontation with the witches. However, the interview is not necessary to the plot, and many Shakespearean authorities believe it was added by some later writer. Note that the rhyme scheme and length of line differ from those used in other scenes involving the witches.

40. **What is the purpose of Scene 6?**

The conversation provides exposition about conditions in Scotland, with particular reference to Macbeth's growing despotism. Here appears the first mention of organized opposition to his rule and, in this way, the scene functions as further preparation for Macbeth's interview with the witches. Macbeth is in trouble and it is to reassure himself that he seeks out those who promised him, as he thought, good fortune.

The remarks about the aid sent from England to Scotland would have had contemporary relish for Shakespeare's audience, for the king of Scotland had recently ascended the throne of England.

Act IV

41. **In Scene 1, why is the witches' chant given in such detail?**

First, it provides "good theater" with its emphasis on the grotesque and the spectacular; meter gives the words particular effect when chanted aloud. Secondly, the chant conjures up an image of the inferno itself.

The bizarre ingredients ("eye of newt," "poisoned entrails," "blindworm's sting") have a haunted quality and prepare for the horror of Macbeth's confrontation with the hags and their apparitions.

42. **Explain the paradox of the apparitions.**

Each apparition seems to provide comfort for Macbeth, but Hecate has told the witches to construct Macbeth's doom. So comfort is couched in riddles. Though Macbeth thinks he understands each apparition, their real meaning is not divulged until later. The scene prepares now for theatrical impact at the play's conclusion.

43. **What is the import of Macbeth's commands about Macduff's family?**

The viciousness of his intent marks Macbeth's moral and mental degeneration. His first murder had a definite, specific purpose: he wanted Duncan's throne. The crime might have been appalling but it was at least comprehensible. The subsequent killing of Banquo was based on a doubtful motive, but it followed a certain logic; he was removing what he considered a threat. This attack on Macduff's family is senseless, bloodshed for the sake of bloodshed.

44. **What attitudes emerge from Lady Macduff's characterization?**

Scene 2 reveals political terror on a very personal level. It is one thing to hear about murder and quite another to see it taking place. The poignancy of Lady Macduff, who has no one to protect her and nowhere to run, sharpens the realization that she poses no threat to Macbeth. Her death is unnecessary.

45. **Who is the messenger?**

The messenger is most probably a disaffected courtier who cannot bear this latest barbarism from Macbeth. He acts to save Lady Macduff's life, and his warning reflects the growing unrest in Scotland and the chaos at court.

Some scholars have suggested that the messenger may be Lady Macbeth, who has become increasingly distraught about the bloodshed she instigated. In the final act, Lady Macbeth shows her distress at murders and moans specifically, "The Thane of Fife had a wife. Where is she now?" in reference to Lady Macduff.

46. **What dramatic elements emerge at the beginning of Scene 3?**

Shakespeare employs foreshadowing and irony. In speaking of the bloodshed at home, Malcolm and Macduff do not realize that they are dealing with a generality which is about to become painfully specific. They discuss the state of affairs in Scotland only minutes before Macduff learns of his personal disaster. Irony is present in Malcolm's thought that Macduff might be Macbeth's spy, since Macduff has dared to leave his wife and children behind in Macbeth's kingdom. Since the family has already been slaughtered, the suspicion has powerful impact.

47. **How does Malcolm test Macduff?**

To probe the depths of Macduff's sincerity, Malcolm accuses himself of various unkingly vices, some of which Macduff can accept. However, when Malcolm says that he would bring disorder to the land, Macduff says that he is not fit to rule. Malcolm then realizes that Macduff's sincerity is unfeigned and that he is a man to be trusted. He tells Macduff of the ruse and explains its necessity. This indicates the treacherous environment Macbeth has created, one which these men must navigate with utmost care.

48. Why do the men discuss the king of England?

These comments have little to do with the structure of the play and were intended in honor of King James, patron and benefactor of Shakespeare's theatrical company.

49. How does Macduff receive the news of his loss?

Macduff has been noted as a man of direct, honest emotion; he was the one who openly questioned Macbeth's explanation of Duncan's death and who avoided the coronation. Now again he shows himself a man of deep feeling.

His reaction is almost unbearably poignant. He is unable to comprehend the scope of the tragedy, and numbly repeats, "My children too? . . . My wife killed too? . . . All my pretty ones? Did you say all?" Malcolm tries to blunt Macduff's suffering with thoughts of revenge, a preparation for the denouement of the final act.

Act V

50. What is Lady Macbeth's mental state in Scene 1?

She has plummeted to melancholy and a deep, prolonged depression. Modern psychiatrists would have specific terms for her malady, but Shakespeare understood the workings of the anguished heart. Lady Macbeth is suffering extreme reaction to the horrors which she has created and shared with her husband.

51. What are conditions in Scotland?

War is imminent, both civil conflict and a foreign one. The Scottish thanes have revolted against Macbeth and, with the aid of the English, Malcolm stands ready to launch his forces. Macbeth faces an uprising from within his state as well as an invasion from without.

There is no doubt that a climax will soon be reached. The foreshadowing by the witches seems to be unraveled here, for Macbeth is fortifying Dunsinane while Malcolm musters his armies at Birnam Wood.

52. **What is Macbeth's mood in Scene 3?**

His attitude as he faces a crucial battle to maintain the throne is a bleak one. He seems like a member of the living dead, unable to feel joy or pain. Though he maintains a purely physical bravery, it is obvious that he would welcome death as indifferently as he continues life.

53. **What is the importance of the camouflage in Scene 4?**

The witches' prophecies have seemed to augur well for Macbeth, but now a hidden meaning is revealed. If Malcolm moves his army, camouflaged with the trees of Birnam Wood, to Macbeth's castle at Dunsinane, a new and contradictory interpretation is suggested. Macbeth has assumed that the witches' prophecy guarantees his success; now events hint at a different outcome.

54. **How does Macbeth receive the news of his wife's death?**

"She should have died hereafter; There would have been a time for such a word." Macbeth's words suggest two interpretations. It might be that in the midst of war, Macbeth has no time to mourn appropriately for her. Or perhaps his words indicate acceptance, since all life must culminate eventually in death. Either way, Macbeth is numb to even this tragic stroke. After horror upon horror, he is no longer capable of even the most elemental emotion.

The famous passage "Tomorrow and tomorrow and tomorrow . . . " is perhaps the most desolate renunciation of life ever put into words. Macbeth negates completely any meaning to existence. Still, at the news of

Malcolm's approach, he summons all his resolution; he is determined to meet his enemy with a show of bravado, even though the information about Birnam Wood shatters his promised invulnerability. Though life now holds no purpose for him, he is determined to play out the game to its end.

55. **What is the importance of Malcolm's speech in Scene 6?**

First, it places Macduff in the forefront in preparation for his role in the final scene. Secondly, Malcolm stresses the significance of British support. To Shakespeare's audiences the mention of English aid to Scotland, depicted on a very personal level by the heroism of Young Siward, would have had a happy connotation.

56. **What is Young Siward's reaction to the name "Macbeth"?**

To Siward it is a synonym for butcher, the foulest sort of criminal. This contrasts sharply the early scenes when the name was coupled with admiring adjectives.

57. **Why does Macbeth speak of playing "the Roman fool"?**

He refuses to take his own life as a means of preventing his enemies' full triumph, as Brutus did when Antony and Octavius defeated him. Macbeth will face his enemies bravely even though the life for which he fights is void of meaning.

58. **How does Macduff reveal Macbeth's doom?**

In divulging the facts of his birth, Macduff reveals the hidden riddle of the prophecies. The duplicity of the witches' promises to Macbeth is now fully apparent. Macduff, delivered in a Caesarian section, was "not of woman born" and can slay Macbeth.

59. **What is the significance of Malcolm's ascension?**

With Macbeth's death and Malcolm's control of the throne, order is restored to Scotland. More important than the political restoration is the renewed operation of moral order: the powers of evil have been overthrown and the forces of good are once more triumphant. The strength of evil was not underestimated, but the power of virtue has ultimately succeeded.

The Play's the Thing: Discussion Questions

Motivation:

1. **What is Macbeth's original attitude toward Duncan?**

At the beginning of the play, Macbeth's predominant feeling toward Duncan is ambition for his throne. He does not hate the man himself, admitting that Duncan has been a good king and has not offended him personally. Duncan's only fault, in Macbeth's eyes, is his possession of the throne.

2. **How does his attitude toward Duncan change?**

After the murder, Macbeth suffers guilt and anguish. The throne he had envied brings him no pleasure; now he envies Duncan the peace in death which Macbeth is unable to achieve in life. "Duncan is in his grave; After life's fitful fever he sleeps well," says Macbeth, knowing that Duncan is beyond the reach of earthly cares.

3. **What is Macbeth's feeling toward Banquo at the beginning of the play?**

At the beginning of the play, Macbeth's attitude toward Banquo is a measure of his emotional well-being and of his attitude toward his fellow-men. Macbeth is relaxed and affable, and the two enjoy mutual respect and friendship. Macbeth is depicted as an upstanding, intelligent and thoughtful citizen, well deserving of the high esteem of his peers.

4. **How does Macbeth alter his attitude toward Banquo?**

After the murder of Duncan, Macbeth is unable to think clearly; a major change occurs in his attitude toward his fellowmen. He sees Banquo only as a possible threat, and determines that he must rid himself of his former friend. The change in Macbeth's feelings toward Banquo reflects a degeneration in his total attitude toward humanity. He no longer views men as individuals but merely as pawns who may affect his throne in one way or another.

5. **What is Macbeth's original attitude toward his wife?**

At the beginning of the play, Macbeth loves his wife dearly but is somewhat subordinate to her. It is she who plans the murder of Duncan and holds him to their plan. She acts as his accomplice, staying calm when he is overwhelmed by the horror of the deed. Almost as soon as he has committed the crime, however, he begins to change. He plans the murder of Banquo without her knowledge and orders Macduff's death without consulting her. Their closeness seems to diminish for, after becoming a murderer, Macbeth seems less and less capable of human responses.

6. **What is Macbeth's final attitude toward his wife?**

By the end of the play, the process of atrophy has numbed Macbeth totally. Everything seems bleak and meaningless to him, and his wife's tortured mind is but part of this joyless world. When the news of her death is brought to him, he is too accustomed to terror to mourn her death. He can only accept it as part of the fate which has hunted him down and vanquished him.

7. **Describe Macbeth's changing attitudes toward the witches.**

At the beginning of the play, Macbeth is startled by the witches and finds their prophecy hard to believe. However, his credulity increases when their first prophecy is brought to fruition: he becomes thane of Cawdor. He tries to ignore the full thrust of their prophecy; but his wife convinces him that, if the prediction is to come true, it must be founded upon his own action. Finally, in order to gain the throne the witches have promised him, he commits an unspeak able murder; to keep the throne he orders the deaths of Banquo, Fleance, Macduff, and Macduff's innocent family.

By the end of the play Macbeth's attitude toward the witches has undergone a painful reversal. He had based all of his actions upon their predictions and trusted them completely. Only at the drama's conclusion does he realize their duplicity. The apparitions which had seemed so clear to him, such obvious portents of success and invulnerability, have a hidden meaning. He finds that he is indeed susceptible, and doom closes in around him.

Philosophy:

1. **What is the relationship between man and nature that underlies Shakespeare's dramas?**

In Renaissance philosophy, the cosmos operated through a grand design; all levels of being were interdependent, functioning as parts of a whole. It was vital that each part work in accordance with its role and station — animal, vegetable, or mineral. At the human level, each class, profession, or individual had to hold its station and perform its assigned duties. To usurp another station would disrupt the entire chain of being, and all nature would react violently. Thus when Macbeth kills his king and seizes the crown, unnatural phenomena occur: darkness covers the day, a falcon is killed by a smaller bird, and the royal stallions devour each other. This is nature's way of protesting a breach in the chain of being. All of nature and mankind will eventually take arms against Macbeth's unnatural assumption of power.

2. **In what way does Macbeth reflect his environment?**

Macbeth's crime reflects the tone of his country. Ancient Scotland, as depicted in the play, seems only recently civilized, still primitive in many ways. It is a nationalist entity, but its unity is threatened by rebellions. Behavior is civilized for the most part, yet superstition still holds strong influence. Macbeth seems to reflect these two facets of his society: he accepts the established code of morals, but he is swayed by primeval urges and ambitions. With his crime, the barbaric undercurrents of his society come to the surface. The fact that Macbeth is defeated and the legitimate heir restored to the throne reflects the hope that society is moving to a more civilized plane.

3. **Is Macbeth's fate determined by destiny or free will?**

Although the witches suggest the role played by destiny, Macbeth is very much the master of his fate. The hags' prophecies, the prodding by an ambitious wife, would have been futile without initiative from Macbeth himself. In the final analysis, it was his decision to take Duncan's life and ultimately bring about his own ruin. Perhaps in no other Shakespearean play is the dilemma so clear-cut and so starkly depicted: Macbeth is given the choice between good and evil, and through his own volition chooses evil.

4. **Does Shakespeare believe that man is punished for the evil he does, rewarded for the good?**

It would be tempting to infer that Shakespeare does take this simplistic view, for Macbeth and his lady die miserably and legitimate order is restored. However, such a generalization is inconsistent with human experience and with many of the incidents of the play itself. Shakespeare could not hold this belief in just reward, for he includes the deaths of the virtuous Duncan, Banquo, Young Siward, and the innocent family of Macduff. Where is their reward for virtue? Despite the quick answer this question prompts, Shakespeare's philosophy is subtle and complex. Evil is usually punished in the end, and, though good men may suffer, virtue is a blessing in and of itself.

It is important to note that Macbeth's punishment is not actually his death, but his life. He is punished for murdering Duncan by the fact that he has become a murderer; like his wife, he is deprived of satisfaction and finally of any emotional response to life at all. Justice may take a circuitous course, but it eventually achieves an even balance.

5. **If the evildoers are killed in the last act, and legitimate powers once more hold sway in Scotland, why is Macbeth a tragedy?**

Though justice is restored in the final act, the drama itself does not focus on Scotland but on the soul of one man. At the play's beginning Macbeth stands upon a pinnacle of achievement. He has a loving wife, the gratitude of his king, the admiration of the entire country. Against this respect he must weigh the temptation of ambition, his tragic flaw. His desire to usurp the throne shows hubris, that overwe'ening pride which spells doom for mankind. Macbeth makes the decision to murder of his own free will, sins, and falls from grace. The tragedy of Macbeth is one of waste: he is a man who has the power to do good yet chooses to do evil.

6. **Malcolm succeeds Macbeth as head of state. What characteristics qualify him for this position?**

The question of who is fit to rule the state is important in *Macbeth*. Malcolm, the ultimate victor, is qualified in every way. Foremost, he is the legitimate heir, named by Duncan as successor to the throne. He also displays signs of manly emotion which Macbeth is incapable of feeling. He mourns with Macduff and with Siward, and seems to share the grief they experience. He is deeply disturbed by Macbeth's despotism, and in conversation with Macduff he reveals his hopes for being a judicious ruler. In addition to measured emotion, he has intelligence. This is displayed even in his shock after his father's death; he keeps his head and arranges to flee the country. (Note the brothers' instinctively cautious plan in contrast to Macduff's fatal negligence in fleeing Scotland without his family.) Malcolm is pragmatically careful in testing Macduff's sincerity, showing his ability to maneuver amidst the treachery Macbeth has fostered. Malcolm's combination of heart and mind ensures that he will be an able ruler.

7. **Macbeth's final commentary on life is contained in the bleak "Tomorrow and tomorrow and tomorrow" speech. Is Macbeth expressing Shakespeare's own viewpoint in these lines?**

This beautifully polished speech is intended to show the aridity of Macbeth's emotions, but it does not reflect Shakespeare's philosophy of life. Macbeth is portrayed throughout the drama as a man who has taken the wrong turn and embraced a set of false values, ensuring his own destruction. Shakespeare very clearly implies that the spiritual malaise which strikes both Macbeth and his accomplice/wife is part of their punishment. Because they have chosen evil and alienated themselves from their fellowmen, they soon lose the ability to feel, to find meaning in life. The joyless desolation of the speech reflects a warning of what life might become for those who respond to forces of evil.

Encore: Vocabulary Words

The main words in the groups below are taken from Macbeth. Mark the letter of the word that is *not* a synonym of the main word.

Act I

1. plight
   a. predicament
   b. predictable
   c. condition

2. brandish
   a. wave
   b. shake
   c. impress

3. rapt
   a. absorbed
   b. dependent
   c. engrossed

4. corporal
   a. physical
   b. official
   c. bodily

5. surmised
   a. imagined
   b. interrupted
   c. assumed

6. peerless
   a. matchless
   b. unbreakable
   c. unequalled

7. chastise
   a. punish
   b. apologize
   c. discipline

8. impedes
   a. hinders
   b. deceives
   c. prevents

9. chalice
   a. cup
   b. platter
   c. grail

10. recompense
    a. payment
    b. promise
    c. requite

Act II

11. augment
    a. enlarge
    b. suggest
    c. increase

12. repose
    a. signal
    b. rest
    c. relaxation

13. prate
   a. babble
   b. chatter
   c. dispute

14. palpable
   a. hateful
   b. tangible
   c. touchable

15. surfeit
   a. overabundance
   b. insistence
   c. excess

16. temperate
   a. moderate
   b. calm
   c. hot

17. unruly
   a. unrestrained
   b. speechless
   c. untamed

18. entreat
   a. request
   b. entertain
   c. implore

19. undivulged
   a. unscarred
   b. unrevealed
   c. hidden

20. consort
   a. associate
   b. treaty
   c. partner

Act III

21. verity
   a. truth
   b. reality
   c. signet

22. dauntless
   a. fearless
   b. dissenting
   c. unafraid

23. valor
   a. amorphous
   b. courage
   c. bravery

24. incensed
   a. infuriated
   b. enraged
   c. invoked

25. bounteous
   a. generous
   b. liberal
   c. unctuous

26. sundry
   a. varied
   b. corroborated
   c. assorted

27. jocund
   a. reputable
   b. cheerful
   c. affable

28. blanched
   a. whitened
   b. paled
   c. maligned

29. profound
   a. deep
   b. defamed
   c. abysmal

30. malevolence
   a. ill will
   b. spite
   c. propitiation

Act IV

31. abjure
   a. renounce
   b. disregard
   c. relinquish

32. gibbet
   a. gallows
   b. gate
   c. scaffold

33. pernicious
   a. spontaneous
   b. destructive
   c. detrimental

34. sear
   a. burn
   b. scald
   c. rescind

35. diminutive
   a. miniature
   b. pungent
   c. tiny

36. judicious
   a. thoughtful
   b. meretricious
   c. sage

37. cistern
   a. reservoir
   b. well
   c. cortex

38. desolate
   a. forsaken
   b. mystique
   c. abandoned

39. redress
   a. amend
   b. atone
   c. anoint

40. discern
   a. detect
   b. discover
   c. dilate

Act V

41. perturbation
   a. agitation
   b. disturbance
   c. fetish

42. murky
   a. obscure
   b. vestry
   c. gloomy

43. recoil
   a. inculcate
   b. retreat
   c. flinch

44. sere
   a. dried
   b. withered
   c. ameliorated

45. upbraid
   a. reprimand
   b. scold
   c. dissemble

46. direness
   a. deposition
   b. viciousness
   c. iniquity

47. tarry
   a. construe
   b. linger
   c. wait

48. clamorous
   a. noisy
   b. raucous
   c. volitional

49. abhor
   a. loathe
   b. relish
   c. despise

50. prowess
   a. bravery
   b. courage
   c. calumny

Improvisation: Student Enrichment

Research:

1. Prepare a brief report on witchcraft through the ages.

2. Write a biographical sketch about King James I of England, including material about his Scottish background and about the "king's touch."

3. Read James Thurber's short story, "The Macbeth Murder Mystery."

4. Read *Macbird* by Barbara Garson, a parody of *Macbeth* dealing with the assassination of John F. Kennedy.

5. Read Shakespeare's *Julius Caesar* and note the part blood plays in that drama. What other comparisons do you note between the two plays?

6. Read Steinbeck's *East of Eden* and compare his belief in men's power to choose between good and evil with the role of decision in *Macbeth*.

Reaction:

1. Read aloud some of the passages in the play which seem most significant to you. Does the way in which they are worded add to the impact of what they say?

2. The play involves a certain fatalism. In your opinion, what role does destiny play in the operation of human affairs?

3. Consider the witches and the apparitions, and then remember the scene in which Macbeth returns after killing Duncan. Which seems to hold the most horror — imagination or reality?

Creation/Composition:

1. Write a television news account of the happenings at the castle when Malcolm leads the rebel force that defeats Macbeth. Include suggestions for visual aids — geneological charts, photographs of individuals, and sketches of battle scenes.

2. Script-write or role-play a eulogy after Macbeth's death given by a compassionate friend who abhors Macbeth's acts yet understands his motives.

3. Write a poem or descriptive essay dealing with the horrors of Lady Macbeth's final mental state.

4. Construct a series of posters using text and illustrations to encourage the Scots to rise up against Macbeth.

5. Write a newspaper review of the first performance of Macbeth in London during the reign of James I.

6. Write a letter to the director of a local theatrical company suggesting that Macbeth be their next production. Give specific reasons for your choice.

Between the Lines: Essay Test

Literal Level

1. What is the turning point of the play?

2. Contrast the immediate reactions of Macbeth and Lady Macbeth to the killing of Duncan.

3. What part do the witches play in the drama?

4. How does the public image of Macbeth change throughout the play?

Interpretive Level

1. What is the turning point of the play?

2. How does Lady Macbeth change throughout the drama?

3. What are the three apparitions the witches use to trick Macbeth and how do they all come true?

4. How does the killing of Lady Macduff differ from the previous killings in what it reveals about Macbeth's personality and conditions in Scotland?

5. At the end of the play, Macbeth is punished for his crimes and the rightful heir ascends the throne. Why then is this play called a tragedy?

Final Curtain: Objective Test

I. True—False

Mark each statement T for True or F for False.

_____ 1. At the end of the play, Malcolm becomes king.

_____ 2. Lady Macbeth takes part in Banquo's murder.

_____ 3. Even though she is warned of treachery, Lady Macduff is killed.

_____ 4. The thanes are loyal to Macbeth to the end.

_____ 5. Macbeth's chief fear is punishment after death.

_____ 6. The witches predict Banquo's heirs will be kings.

_____ 7. Banquo faints after the killing of Duncan.

_____ 8. Lady Macbeth does not see Banquo's ghost.

_____ 9. Malcolm knows Macbeth better than Duncan does.

_____10. The witches have human form.

_____11. The doctor says Lady Macbeth suffers from a fatal illness.

_____12. Macbeth and his wife love each other deeply.

_____13. Macbeth's explanation of Duncan's death satisfies the king's sons.

_____14. Duncan is suspicious of Macbeth.

_____15. Remorse ruins Lady Macbeth's enjoyment of success.

II. Multiple Choice

Choose the best answer to complete each statement.

16. The porter scene is the play's
    a. beginning.
    b. comic relief.
    c. climax.

17. As king, Macbeth is
    a. brutal.
    b. wise.
    c. gentle.

18. The former thane of Cawdor had been
    a. a traitor.
    b. Duncan's son.
    c. brother to Macbeth.

19. Macbeth meets death
    a. as a physical coward.
    b. as a repentant.
    c. with desperate courage.

20. Banquo's son is
    a. Fleance.
    b. Sinel.
    c. Macdonwald.

21. The "third murderer" is sent by
    a. Macbeth.
    b. Banquo.
    c. Lady Macbeth.

22. Malcolm's invasion is launched from
    a. France.
    b. Norway.
    c. England.

23. At his wife's death, Macbeth
    a. swears revenge.
    b. accepts fate.
    c. vows to change.

24. Macbeth is killed by
    a. Malcolm.
    b. Macduff.
    c. Fleance.

25. Duncan's murderer is
    a. Lady Macbeth.
    b. Macbeth.
    c. Banquo.

26. Duncan's death is blamed on
    a. the grooms.
    b. Norwegians.
    c. the doctor.

27. Lady Macbeth receives a diamond from
    a. Macbeth.
    b. Malcolm.
    c. Duncan.

28. Malcolm tests the loyalty of
    a. Macduff.
    b. Banquo.
    c. Sinel.

29. Duncan's sons are
    a. Ross and Malcolm.
    b. Malcolm and Donalbain.
    c. Macduff and Siward.

30. Lady Macbeth becomes
    a. a sleepwalker.
    b. a mute.
    c. an insomniac.

31. Macbeth's evil side is associated with
    a. royalty.
    b. the color blue.
    c. night and darkness.

32. Hecate is linked to
    a. the witches.
    b. the English nobility.
    c. the Scottish nobility.

33. The wife of the thane of Fife is
    a. Lady Macbeth.
    b. Hecate.
    c. Lady Macduff.

34. After Duncan's death, Macbeth finds killing
    a. impossible.
    b. not worth it.
    c. often necessary.

35. For his bravery and loyalty Macbeth becomes
    a. king of Scotland.
    b. thane of Fife.
    c. thane of Cawdor.

III. Matching

A. Match the character with the proper description.

_____36. the porter   a. praised for his healing touch
_____37. Macdonwald   b. tells Fleance to excape
_____38. Duncan   c. talks of an equivocator
_____39. Banquo   d. praises Macbeth's castle
_____40. King James   e. a traitor to Scotland

B. Match each place with the proper description.

_____41. England   a. Macbeth's original estate
_____42. Birnam   b. refuge for Malcolm
_____43. Glamis   c. at war with Scotland
_____44. Norway   d. a forest
_____45. Inverness   e. site of Duncan's murder

C. Match each item with its description.

_____46. the dagger
_____47. eye of newt
_____48. a man not born of woman
_____49. Banquo's ghost
_____50. a bloodstain

     a. appears to Lady Macbeth
     b. Macduff
     c. attends the banquet
     d. appears before Duncan's murder
     e. part of witches' brew